Equipped for Mission

A Study of Acts 13–28

By Matthew Allen

Published by
Spiritbuilding Publishers
9700 Ferry Road, Waynesville, Ohio 45068

EQUIPPED FOR MISSION
A Study of Acts 13–28
By Matthew Allen

ISBN: 978–1–964–80563–4

Spiritbuilding
PUBLISHERS
spiritbuilding.com

Table of Contents

Introduction

The book of Acts recounts how the gospel spread from Jerusalem to the farthest corners of the earth. It records the stories of ordinary people empowered by the Holy Spirit, facing opposition, hardship, and uncertainty, yet never losing sight of their mission. Each chapter reminds us that when God calls, He also equips.

This class, *Equipped for the Mission*, traces the apostle Paul's journey through the final chapters of Acts. These last scenes illustrate how faith persists when life doesn't go as planned. From conflict and imprisonment to storms and shipwrecks, Paul learns that the Spirit of God supplies everything needed for faithful service. His courage, humility, and commitment to Christ serve as a model for every Christian striving to serve faithfully in a changing and often hostile world.

Each lesson in this study highlights how God equips His people through various means: hardship, leadership, courage, suffering, perseverance, and opportunity. The emphasis is on God's faithfulness, not Paul's greatness; the same Spirit who supported him continues to empower us. Every passage shows how God transforms obstacles into open doors, setbacks into service, and weakness into strength.

This workbook is designed for group study and discussion. Each lesson includes:

- Biblical exposition that draws out the key truths of the text.
- Reflection and discussion questions to encourage application.
- Key summary points that highlight what God is teaching.
- A memory verse and weekly challenge to carry truth into daily life.

The purpose of this study is simple: to show you that the mission of Acts continues through us. The gospel still moves forward, often through hardship, always through faith. Wherever we are, whatever our circumstances, God calls us to proclaim the kingdom of God "with all boldness and without hindrance."

The story that began in the book of Acts is still being written in our generation. The same Spirit who guided Paul through storms and prisons now works in the church today, equipping every Christian to serve, to endure, and to lead others to Christ.

Matthew Allen

November 2025

How to Use This Book

This workbook is created to help you explore Scripture and apply what you learn. Each lesson guides you through a section of Acts, illustrating how the Spirit of God equips His followers for faith, endurance, and service. Use this material as both a study guide and a discussion resource.

1. Read the Passage Carefully

Begin each lesson by reading the assigned Scripture. Read it more than once, slowly and prayerfully. Let the text speak before turning to the commentary. Keep a notebook or margin notes to capture insights, questions, and recurring themes.

2. Study Each Section

Every lesson includes three main study points. These sections explain what happens in the passage, what it means, and how it applies. Move through each section thoughtfully. Look for what it teaches about God, the gospel, and the life of faith.

3. Reflect and Discuss

Use the reflection questions at the end of each lesson to think personally and to guide group discussion. The questions are written to draw out practical application and spiritual growth, not just information. Take time to listen and share honestly.

4. Review the Key Truths

Each lesson concludes with a summary of key truths. These brief statements capture the main principles to remember. They are ideal for quick review or class recap.

5. Memorize and Apply

The memory verse / weekly challenge connects the lesson to daily life. Memorize the verse and take the challenge seriously. Each challenge offers a simple way to live out the week's truth: through prayer, encouragement, service, or witness.

6. Build Week by Week

The lessons follow Paul's journey from ministry to imprisonment to mission in Rome. Each week builds on the one before it. As the story unfolds, watch how God's faithfulness carries His servant through every circumstance.

7. Keep the Focus on the Mission

This workbook is not just about Paul's story: it's about ours. God still equips His people today. Use these studies to strengthen your faith, grow in confidence, and renew your commitment to the mission of Christ.

He proclaimed the kingdom of God and taught about the Lord Jesus Christ with all boldness and without hindrance.
Acts 28:31

Equipped for a Mission:
The Church at Antioch
Acts 13:1–12

Now in the church at Antioch there were prophets and teachers: Barnabas, Simeon who was called Niger, Lucius of Cyrene, Manaen, a close friend of Herod the tetrarch, and Saul. As they were worshiping the Lord and fasting, the Holy Spirit said, "Set apart for me Barnabas and Saul for the work to which I have called them." Then, after they had fasted, prayed, and laid hands on them, they sent them off.

Acts 13:1–3

Class Overview: Acts 13:1–12 records the moment when the gospel begins to spread beyond the familiar borders of Judea and Samaria. From the lively and diverse church in Antioch, the Holy Spirit calls Barnabas and Saul to take Christ's message to the Gentile world. This lesson explores how God equipped that congregation through worship, fasting, and prayer to become a sending church. We will see how obedience to the Spirit's direction led to the first major missionary journey and how God's power worked through ordinary believers to achieve extraordinary results.

Class Objectives: By the end of this class, you should be able to—

1. Describe the spiritual and cultural setting of the church at Antioch and why it became a model for mission.
2. Explain how worship, fasting, and prayer prepared the Antioch Christians to hear the Spirit's call.
3. Understand that God's mission is directed by the Holy Spirit, not human planning or ambition.
4. Recognize that gospel work involves both opportunity and opposition and that the Spirit provides strength to overcome.
5. Identify ways today's church can imitate Antioch by sending, supporting, and serving in the mission of Christ.

Introduction

THE STORY OF ACTS 13 MARKS A TURNING POINT in the book of Acts and in the history of the church. Up to this point, the gospel had spread from Jerusalem to Judea and Samaria, mainly through the efforts of Peter and other apostles. But beginning in Acts 13, the center of God's mission shifts to a new city, Antioch, and to new messengers, Barnabas and Saul. From here, the message of Christ begins to move out to the ends of the earth.

Antioch was a remarkable congregation. It was made up of Jews and Gentiles, rich and poor, leaders and servants. They had already shown a generous heart by sending aid to believers in Judea during a famine. More than that, they had a deep spiritual focus. Luke tells us they were worshiping and fasting when the Holy Spirit gave direction. Their hearts were open to God's will. They were not just maintaining what they had; they were seeking what God wanted next.

When the Spirit spoke, He didn't call the church to comfort but to commission. Two of their best men, Barnabas and Saul, were to be set apart and sent out. This was divine direction. The church obeyed immediately. They prayed, laid hands on the men, and released them for the mission. What followed changed the world.

The church's mission starts with worship. When God's people focus on Him, He gives them a vision for others. Antioch shows what it means to be a sending church. Antioch shows what it means to be a sending church: one that listens to the Spirit, values the gospel above its own convenience, and gladly gives its best for the sake of Christ.? Every congregation today faces the same challenge: will we cling tightly to our comforts, or will we open our hands and let God use us to reach the world?

Historical Background

Antioch of Syria was one of the great cities of the ancient world. It ranked third in size after Rome and Alexandria. It served as a crossroads of culture, trade, and religion. Situated about 300 miles north of Jerusalem, it was a place where East met West. The city was populated with people from all backgrounds, and its moral climate reflected the paganism of the Roman world. Yet, this unlikely location became the headquarters for gospel outreach to the Gentile nations.

The church there began when ordinary Christians, scattered by persecution in Jerusalem, started preaching the word (Acts 11:19–21). Some of them, men from Cyprus and Cyrene, began sharing the gospel with both Greeks and Jews, and "a great number believed and turned to the Lord." When Barnabas was sent from Jerusalem to see what was happening, he rejoiced and brought Saul from Tarsus to help teach. For a year, they worked side by side, strengthening the young congregation. It was in Antioch that disciples were first called Christians, a name that highlighted their loyalty to Christ rather than any nationality or background.

By the time Acts 13 begins, the Antioch church had become strong in teaching, unified in leadership, and generous in heart. They had already sent financial aid to Judea during the famine, demonstrating compassion for others. Now they were sending people, missionaries, to spread the gospel into new territories. In this way, Antioch became the example for every future missionary church.

A Spirit-Filled Church (13:1–2)

The church at Antioch was blessed with a strong group of teachers and prophets. Luke lists five men who led the congregation: Barnabas, Simeon called Niger, Lucius of Cyrene, Manaen, and Saul. This short list says much about the kind of church Antioch had become. It was diverse. It was united. It was growing in grace. These men came from different regions, races, and backgrounds. One had been raised with Herod the tetrarch, another came from North Africa, and others were Jewish believers who had embraced Jesus as the Messiah. Yet they were serving side by side in harmony.

That unity was not by accident. It flowed from worship. Luke says, *As they were worshiping the Lord and fasting, the Holy Spirit said* (v. 2). This tells us something important about the life of the church. The Antioch Christians were not simply running programs or holding meetings;

they were ministering to the Lord. Their focus was upward before it was outward. They were seeking God's will through prayer, fasting, and devotion.

When the Spirit spoke, He found a congregation ready to listen. A Spirit-filled church is one that makes room for God to speak through His word, prayer, and humble, eager hearts. Antioch reminds us that the power for mission doesn't come from plans or committees; it begins in worship. Before the church can send, it must first bow before the Lord who sends.

Every time we gather in authentic worship, we prepare ourselves for mission. Worship aligns our hearts with God's purpose. It reminds us who the mission belongs to and gives us the courage to obey. The Antioch church shows us that when God's people seek Him first, the Spirit always directs them outward, to a world that still needs Jesus.

A Spirit-Directed Mission (13:2–3)

When the Holy Spirit spoke, His message was simple but life-changing: *Set apart for me Barnabas and Saul for the work to which I have called them.* (v. 2). God had a specific task in mind, and He chose these two men to carry it out. They didn't volunteer themselves. They didn't launch a personal mission. They were called by the Spirit, recognized by the church, and sent with prayer.

This is how all true missions begin. It doesn't start with human plans but with God's initiative. The church did not decide to send missionaries because it wanted to expand. They acted in obedience to what the Spirit revealed. After fasting and praying, they laid hands on Barnabas and Saul and released them to the work. That gesture showed both their blessing and their partnership. The church at Antioch was not losing two of its best leaders; it was sending them as an extension of its own faith and work.

Notice the pattern here: worship → listening → obedience. God still uses this pattern today. When His people worship sincerely, He guides them toward His mission. When they listen humbly, He provides clarity.

When they obey, He multiplies the work. The Antioch church shows us that being "Spirit-led" is not about emotion or impulse: it's about submission. It's the willingness to go where God sends and to release what He asks for.

Every congregation faces the same calling. Sometimes God calls us to move into new territory personally. Other times, He calls us to send and support those who go. Either way, obedience requires faith. To be a Spirit-led church is to hold everything, our resources, our time, our people, open before God and say, "Use us for Your purpose." That's when the true mission begins.

A Spirit-Empowered Message (Acts 13:4–12)

After being sent out by the church, Barnabas and Saul set sail for Cyprus. This island was familiar territory for Barnabas; it was his home. This was the natural place to begin. But what matters most is not geography; it is obedience. Luke says plainly, *so being sent out by the Holy Spirit, they went down to Seleucia and from there they sailed to Cyprus.* (v. 4). The mission that began in worship now moves forward in power.

As they preached throughout the island, they faced both opportunity and opposition. In Paphos, they met two men who represent the clash of truth and deceit: Sergius Paulus, a Roman official open to hearing God's word, and Elymas, a magician who tried to turn him away from the faith. Here we learn that gospel work is never without resistance. Wherever truth advances, Satan pushes back. But God equips His servants for such moments.

Paul, filled with the Holy Spirit, confronted Elymas directly: *You are full of all kinds of deceit and trickery… will you ever stop perverting the straight paths of the Lord?* (v. 10) The man who once persecuted the church now stood firm for Christ. His boldness did not come from natural strength; it came from the Spirit. God struck Elymas blind for a time, showing that the power of darkness cannot stand against the light of Christ. When Sergius Paulus saw what happened, he believed, amazed at the teaching of the Lord.

Here we see a spiritual reality. The gospel always advances through conflict. Faith grows when believers trust God's word and stand firm in truth. A Spirit-empowered message does not rely on clever speech or a forceful personality. It depends on the Spirit's power working through people willing to speak up for Jesus.

When we face opposition or doubt, we can remember that the same Spirit who filled Paul lives in us. God still opens doors, still silences the enemy, and still changes hearts through His Word. Our task is to stay faithful, speak truth, and let God do what only He can do.

Lesson Summary and Reflection

Key truths from Syrian Antioch:

- Mission begins in worship.
- The Spirit, not human planning, directs the work.
- God's power overcomes opposition.
- Sending is an act of faith, not loss.
- Every member participates in the mission.

The story of Antioch reminds us of what God can do through ordinary Christians who are willing to listen and obey. Their strength was not in size, wealth, or position; it was in their surrender to the Spirit. As they worshiped, the Lord gave direction. As they prayed, He gave power. As they sent their best, He expanded His mission.

Every church today is called to live out the same pattern. The gospel advances when God's people focus upward in worship and outward in mission. Antioch teaches us that sending is not losing; it's multiplying. Their obedience opened a new chapter in God's plan to reach the world, and the same Spirit is still at work through His church today.

When we see our local congregation as a base for mission, everything changes. Worship becomes preparation. Giving becomes a partnership. Prayer becomes participation. And every brother or sister, whether staying or going, becomes part of God's story to make Christ known.

Memory Verse and Weekly Challenge

As they were worshiping the Lord and fasting, the Holy Spirit said, "Set apart for me Barnabas and Saul for the work to which I have called them."
Acts 13:2

Weekly Challenge: Spend time in prayer this week, asking God where He might be calling you to serve or send.

For Reflection

1. What qualities made the church at Antioch ready for God's call?

    _____

    _____

    _____

2. How does worship prepare us to hear and obey the Spirit?

    _____

    _____

    _____

3. What does this story teach us about letting go of comfort and security for the sake of the mission?

    _____

    _____

    _____

4. In what ways might God be calling you or your congregation to "send" today?

    _____

    _____

    _____

5. How can you personally live more like a Spirit-filled, Spirit-sent disciple this week?

    _____

    _____

    _____

Equipped to Preach Christ: The Church in Pisidian Antioch

Acts 13:13–52

Therefore, let it be known to you, brothers and sisters, that through this man forgiveness of sins is being proclaimed to you. Everyone who believes is justified through him from everything that you could not be justified from through the law of Moses. (Acts 13:38–39).

Class Overview: Acts 13:13–52 records Paul's first sermon and stands as one of the clearest examples of gospel preaching in the New Testament. Speaking in the synagogue at Pisidian Antioch, Paul explained how all of Israel's history pointed to Jesus, the promised Savior who offers forgiveness and justification through His death and resurrection. This lesson shows how the Holy Spirit enables believers to proclaim Christ with clarity, courage, and compassion, even when faced with rejection. Through Paul's example, we learn that the power of the gospel does not depend on human approval but on God's truth faithfully shared.

Class Objectives: By the end of this class, you should be able to—

1. Explain how Paul used Scripture to connect Israel's story to Jesus as the Messiah.
2. Summarize the main points of Paul's sermon and its emphasis on forgiveness through Christ.
3. Recognize that gospel preaching often brings both acceptance and opposition.
4. Describe how the Holy Spirit empowers believers to speak with courage and endure with joy.
5. Apply Paul's example by sharing the gospel with others in simple, Scripture-centered ways.

Introduction:

When Paul and Barnabas set out from Antioch, they entered the unknown. The comfort of their home church was behind them. Ahead, there were rough roads, unfamiliar cities, and spiritual opposition. Yet, they moved forward confidently because the Holy Spirit had called them, and the message they carried was worth every risk.

Their journey first took them across the island of Cyprus and then north into the mountainous region of Galatia. It was there, in Pisidian Antioch, that Paul delivered his first recorded sermon. His message was simple and clear. It was a straightforward proclamation that God had fulfilled His promises by sending Jesus, who died for our sins and was raised from the dead. Through Him, forgiveness and freedom are available to everyone who believes.

This sermon serves as a model for every Christian seeking to share the gospel. Paul didn't rely on eloquence or emotion; he opened the Scriptures and demonstrated how all of history pointed to Christ. His emphasis was on Jesus: His identity, His mission, and His resurrection.

But not everyone welcomed the message. Some rejoiced, while others rejected it. Paul and Barnabas faced jealousy, opposition, and persecution, yet they refused to stay silent. Their boldness stemmed from deep conviction and trust in God's word. Even when driven out of town, they left behind new believers filled with joy and the Holy Spirit.

This story reminds us that gospel work always involves both triumph and trial. The same Spirit who equipped Paul and Barnabas to preach in Pisidian Antioch equips us today. Our mission is the same. We must proclaim Christ with clarity, courage, and compassion, trusting God to bring the results.

Historical Background

Pisidian Antioch was a Roman colony in the mountainous region of southern Galatia, near present-day Turkey. It was not the same city as Syrian Antioch, where Paul and Barnabas started their journey. This Antioch was an important city along the *Via Sebaste*, a key trade route connecting the interior of Asia Minor with the coast. Due to its location and Roman influence, the city drew soldiers, merchants, and settlers from all over the empire.

The trip there was difficult. To reach Pisidian Antioch, Paul and Barnabas had to go through rough terrain and dangerous mountain passes. Bandits were frequent, and the road was tough. Paul later mentioned the challenges he faced during his travels in Galatia (2 Corinthians 11:26). Still, those hardships helped shape and prepare God's servants for endurance.

The city had a sizable Jewish population and a synagogue that also attracted many Gentile "God-fearers" (non-Jews who respected Israel's Scriptures and worshiped the one true God). This diverse crowd created fertile ground for the gospel. Paul followed his usual pattern: he went first to the synagogue, stood up to read from the Scriptures, and used that moment to proclaim Jesus as the fulfillment of God's promises to Israel.

Pisidian Antioch became a key turning point in Paul's ministry. Here, he first faced open rejection from Jewish leaders who opposed the gospel message. Yet it was also here that the mission to the Gentiles took clearer form. As the Jews turned away, Paul and Barnabas boldly declared, *We are turning to the Gentiles.* (Acts 13:46). From that moment, the gospel began spreading with new momentum across the Roman world.

God often opens new doors through difficulty. The same Spirit who guided Paul through danger and rejection still equips us today to carry the message of Christ into challenging and unfamiliar places.

Equipped to Preach the Word (13:13–25)

When Paul and Barnabas arrived in Pisidian Antioch, they followed a pattern that would shape much of Paul's ministry: first, go to the synagogue and speak to those familiar with the Scriptures. On the Sabbath, after the reading from the Law and the Prophets, synagogue rulers invited Paul to share a word of encouragement. Paul stood up, gestured, and began to speak. What followed was a powerful, Spirit-led message that highlighted God's faithfulness throughout Israel's history and pointed directly to Jesus as the promised Savior.

Paul starts with what his listeners already believe. He reminds them how God chose Israel, led them out of Egypt, and gave them David, a man after His own heart. Then he states that, from David's descendants, God sent the Savior, Jesus, to Israel, as He had promised. In doing so, Paul shows that the gospel is not a new religion but the fulfillment of everything God has been doing from the start.

Notice how God prepared Paul for this moment. Paul had a deep understanding of the Scriptures, and the Spirit gave him wisdom to link them to Christ. His sermon wasn't based on opinion but on revelation. This is how every messenger of God should approach the word. We speak with clarity, humility, and confidence in what God has already spoken.

Paul also honored the role of John the Baptist, demonstrating how John's ministry prepared the way for Christ by calling people to repentance. In every generation, God raises voices to prepare hearts to receive His truth. Paul understood that he was now part of that same mission: to help people see how God's promises are fulfilled in Jesus.

God still equips His people to speak His word at the right time and place. The gospel takes hold when we start where people are; building bridges from what they know to what they need to learn about Christ. Every Christian, whether standing before a crowd or sitting across a table, can learn from Paul's example: begin with the story of God's faithfulness and point people to Jesus, the Savior He has provided.

Equipped to Proclaim the Gospel (13:26–37)

After tracing Israel's history, Paul turned to the heart of his message: the good news about Jesus Christ. He addressed his listeners as "brothers and sisters, children of Abraham's race, and those among you who fear God." His tone was respectful yet direct. He wanted everyone in the room, Jew and Gentile alike, to understand that the message of salvation was for them.

Paul proclaimed that the people of Jerusalem and their leaders had fulfilled the prophets' words by condemning Jesus to death. They didn't recognize Him as the Messiah, even though the Scriptures they read every Sabbath pointed to Him. Without realizing it, their rejection accomplished God's plan. Jesus was crucified, buried, and then raised from the dead, just as God had promised.

This was not just a rumor or speculation. Paul stated that many witnesses had seen the risen Lord and could testify to it. The resurrection proved that Jesus was the promised Savior and Son of God. It confirmed that death had been defeated and that forgiveness was now available for everyone who believes.

To demonstrate that this was not a new message, Paul quoted from Psalm 2, Isaiah 55, and Psalm 16. These passages had long pointed to God's promise of a holy one who would not see decay. David died and was buried, Paul reasoned, but Jesus was raised and lives forever. In Him, the promises made to the fathers were fulfilled.

Paul's boldness stemmed from his conviction that the gospel is both accurate and trustworthy. He didn't depend on emotion or debate. Instead, he relied on Scripture and the resurrection as his authority. The Spirit empowered him to proclaim the gospel clearly, demonstrating that salvation is not earned but received through faith in Jesus Christ.

This same calling is ours. The gospel remains unchanged, along with its power. God continues to equip His people to declare it, i.e., to show others that forgiveness and new life are possible through the risen Lord. Whether we speak to one person or many, our confidence does not rest in our skill but in the truth of what God has done in Christ.

Equipped to Persevere in Mission (13:38–52)

Paul's sermon ended with an invitation and a warning. He proclaimed, *Therefore, let it be known to you ... that through this man forgiveness of sins is being proclaimed to you. Everyone who believes is justified through him from everything that you could not be justified from through the law of Moses.* (vv. 38–39). These words captured the heart of the gospel: forgiveness and justification through Christ alone. What the law could never accomplish, grace has done.

Paul's message elicited mixed reactions. Many in the synagogue were deeply touched. As the meeting ended, they begged to hear more the following Sabbath. Some Jews and God-fearing Gentiles followed Paul and Barnabas, who encouraged them to remain in the grace of God. The gospel had taken root in their hearts.

But when the next Sabbath arrived, almost the entire city gathered to hear the word of the Lord, and that's when jealousy flared up. Some Jewish leaders couldn't stand the attention Paul was getting. They began to oppose him and stir up trouble. Yet Paul didn't back down. Filled with courage, he said, *it was necessary that the word of God be spoken to you first. Since you reject it… we are turning to the Gentiles.* (v. 46)

That statement marked a pivotal moment in the church's mission. The gospel was never intended to be limited to one group of people. God's plan had always been that all nations would hear about His salvation. When the Gentiles received this message, they rejoiced and honored the word of the Lord, and many believed. Opposition could not stop the message, as it only propelled it further.

Even after being driven out of the region, Paul and Barnabas left behind a thriving group of new Christians. Luke ends the story by saying, *And the disciples were filled with joy and the Holy Spirit.* (v. 52). That is the mark of a Spirit-equipped church: joy amid hardship and faith that endures when rejected.

Perseverance in mission means trusting that God is working even when the results seem uncertain. Some will resist, others will believe, but the word of God always bears fruit. Like Paul and Barnabas, we are called to keep speaking, keep serving, and keep rejoicing in the power of the gospel.

Lesson Summary and Reflection

Key Truths from Pisidian Antioch:

- God equips His servants to proclaim Christ with clarity and conviction.
- The gospel fulfills God's promises and centers on the death and resurrection of Jesus.
- Forgiveness and justification come only through faith in Christ, not through the works of the law.
- Opposition cannot silence God's word; it often becomes the means of spreading it further.
- Joy in the Holy Spirit sustains believers even when the world rejects the message.

Paul's first recorded sermon in Pisidian Antioch exemplifies gospel-centered preaching. He began with what his audience knew, the history of God's relationship with Israel, and led them to understand that Jesus is the fulfillment of all God's promises. Throughout, his message focused on Christ's death and resurrection as the foundation for forgiveness and justification.

Gospel preaching isn't about personality, emotion, or eloquence. It is about truth. The same Spirit who empowered Paul to proclaim Christ equips us today to speak clearly and confidently about what God has done in Jesus. When the message of grace is preached faithfully, some will believe and rejoice, while others will reject and resist. Yet even in rejection, God's purpose moves forward.

The final image of the disciples "filled with joy and the Holy Spirit" (v. 52) captures the core of this lesson. True mission is maintained not by results but through a relationship with the Lord and His Spirit. God equips His people not just to deliver the message but to persevere in it happily. As long as there are hearts that haven't heard, our mission remains the same: proclaim Christ, rely on the power of His Word, and rejoice that the gospel still transforms lives.

Memory Verse and Weekly Challenge

Therefore, my brothers and sisters,
know that through this man forgiveness of sins is being proclaimed to you.
Acts 13:38

Weekly Challenge: Share the message of forgiveness in Jesus with one person. You don't need to know everything; tell them what God has done for you. Pray for courage and trust that the same Spirit who equipped Paul will give you the words to speak.

For Reflection

1. How did Paul's understanding of Israel's history prepare him to preach the gospel effectively in Pisidian Antioch?

    _____

    _____

    _____

2. What stands out to you about how Paul connected the OT to Jesus?

    _____

    _____

    _____

3. Why is the resurrection central to the gospel message, and how does it strengthen your faith today?

    _____

    _____

    _____

4. What can we learn from Paul's courage and persistence in the face of jealousy and opposition?

    _____

    _____

    _____

5. How can your congregation cultivate the same boldness and joy that Paul and Barnabas showed in their mission?

    _____

    _____

    _____

Equipping Through Suffering: Paul and Barnabas in Lystra
Acts 14:1–28

It is necessary to go through many hardships to enter the kingdom of God.
Acts 14:22

Class Overview: Acts 14 shows that suffering isn't a sign of failure but a part of God's plan to strengthen His followers. As Paul and Barnabas traveled through Iconium, Lystra, and Derbe, they experienced both success and intense opposition. Yet, through every challenge, God equipped them to stand firm, stay humble, and persevere with joy. This lesson reminds us that hardship is one of God's most effective tools for shaping faith, preparing His people, and demonstrating the power of the gospel to endure in all circumstances.

Class Objectives:

By the end of this class, you should be able to:

1. Summarize the main events in Acts 14 and how Paul and Barnabas responded to persecution.
2. Explain how God uses suffering to mature and equip believers for continued ministry.
3. Identify the dangers of pride in moments of success and how humility protects faith.
4. Recognize that perseverance and endurance are essential qualities of true discipleship.
5. Apply the example of Paul and Barnabas by viewing personal hardship as an opportunity to glorify God and strengthen others.

Introduction

THE ROAD TO MISSION IS NOT ALWAYS SMOOTH. Acts 14 reminds us that the same Spirit who empowers us to serve also sustains us when the path grows rough. Paul and Barnabas had seen great success in Pisidian Antioch, but success was followed by suffering. As they traveled on to Iconium, Lystra, and Derbe, they met both open hearts and angry mobs. Some believed the message; others tried to silence it. Yet through it all, they kept preaching, kept moving, and kept trusting God.

Acts 14 reveals that suffering is not a setback in God's work; it is part of it. The gospel progresses through struggle as much as through peace. God uses opposition to refine His servants and deepen their reliance on Him. Paul and Barnabas didn't give up when they faced opposition, misunderstanding, or even stoning. They got back up, continued the work, and encouraged others to do the same.

The story of Lystra also exposes how quickly human praise can turn to hostility. One day, the people tried to worship Paul and Barnabas as gods; the next, they stoned Paul and dragged him out of the city. Yet the mission continued. God's servants learned that the same Spirit who calls and sends also comforts and sustains.

We need to see hardship through the same lens. When we face rejection, criticism, or pain for doing what is right, we are not abandoned; we are being equipped. The Spirit who helped Paul stand back up helps us stand, too. Through suffering, God strengthens faith, shapes character, and prepares His people for greater service in His kingdom.

Historical Background

After leaving Pisidian Antioch, Paul and Barnabas traveled southeast about 80 miles to Iconium, a large and prosperous city in the region of Lycaonia. It was a mixed community of Greeks, Jews, and Romans. As was their pattern, they began preaching in the synagogue, and many believed. But again, opposition arose. Some Jews stirred up hostility and divided the city. The apostles stayed as long as they could, boldly speaking for the Lord, until the tension grew so great that they were forced to leave.

They next came to Lystra, a small, rural town with little Jewish presence. There may not have even been a synagogue there. The people spoke in the local Lycaonian dialect and practiced pagan worship. When Paul healed a man who had been crippled from birth, the crowd was amazed. They shouted that the gods had come down in human form and began calling Barnabas "Zeus" and Paul "Hermes." The priest of Zeus even brought oxen and garlands to offer sacrifices to them.

This misunderstanding shows how much pagan religion influenced the people's thinking. According to their myths, the gods sometimes appeared as men, so they thought the miracle meant divine visitors had arrived. Paul and Barnabas tore their clothes in distress, begging the people to turn from idols to the living God, who made heaven and earth. But soon, Jewish opponents from Antioch and Iconium arrived, turned the crowd against them, and Paul was stoned and left for dead outside the city.

Incredibly, Paul survived. The believers gathered around him, and he got up and returned to the city. The next day, he and Barnabas went to Derbe, where they made many disciples. Then, instead of heading directly home, they retraced their steps—going back to Lystra, Iconium, and Antioch to strengthen the new believers and appoint elders in each church.

The events in Acts 14 illustrate both the risks and the resolve involved in early gospel work. These cities, each facing its own difficulties, became training grounds where Paul and Barnabas learned to persevere. Through persecution, confusion, and hardship, God equipped them to trust Him more fully and to inspire others to do the same.

Equipped to Stand Firm in Opposition (14:1–7)

Paul and Barnabas began their work in Iconium much like they had in other cities: by going to the synagogue and preaching the word of God. Luke records that *a great number of both Jews and Greeks believed* (v. 1). The gospel once again proved its power to unite people from different backgrounds. Wherever the message of Christ is preached with boldness, hearts are changed.

But opposition quickly arose. Some Jews who refused to believe stirred up hostility and poisoned others' minds against the brothers. Instead of fleeing, Paul and Barnabas stayed. Luke says they *remained there a long time and spoke boldly for the Lord* (v. 3). They understood that truth is worth defending and that perseverance often brings quiet victories in hostile places. God confirmed their message by enabling them to perform signs and wonders, demonstrating His presence and power.

Eventually, the city was divided; some supported the apostles, while others sided with their enemies. A plan to mistreat and stone them was formed, so they fled to the surrounding region of Lycaonia, including Lystra and Derbe. However, even as they departed, they were not retreating out of fear. They left to continue their preaching rather than to escape trouble. And Luke says, *there they kept on preaching the gospel.* (v. 7)

That simple statement captures the core of faithful endurance. No matter where they went, they kept teaching. The Holy Spirit had empowered them with courage that outlasted criticism and strength that overcame fear. They understood that opposition does not mean failure—it means the message is being heard.

Every Christian will face opposition in some form. Faithfulness often causes conflict. The key is not to give up but to stay rooted in the Lord's purpose. God does not guarantee ease, but He does guarantee endurance. When we remain firm in truth, even under pressure, He uses our perseverance to draw others to the gospel.

Equipped to Remain Humble in Success (14:8–18)

In Lystra, Paul and Barnabas encountered a man who had been crippled since birth and had never walked. As Paul preached, he noticed a willingness to believe in the man's face. Paul called out, *"Stand up on your feet!"* and the man immediately leapt to his feet and began walking. The miracle was undeniable. The crowd erupted in excitement—yet what happened next revealed how easily people can misunderstand God's message.

The people shouted in their local language, *'The gods have come down to us in human form!'* They called Barnabas "Zeus" and Paul 'Hermes' because Paul was the main speaker. Soon, the priest of Zeus brought oxen and garlands to offer sacrifices to them. To the people of Lystra, this appeared to be an act of gratitude and worship. To Paul and Barnabas, it was a disaster. They tore their clothes in grief and rushed into the crowd, pleading with them to stop.

Their response showed genuine humility. Instead of accepting praise or enjoying the attention, they credited all glory to God. They exclaimed, *we are people also, just like you!* and urged the crowd to turn away from useless idols toward the living God who made heaven and earth. Paul's brief sermon at that moment offers a glimpse of how he addressed Gentiles with little knowledge of Scripture. He started not with prophecy but with creation, illustrating that the one true God is the source of life and blessing.

Even with these words, the people barely held back from offering sacrifices. This moment of misguided worship reminds us how quickly admiration can turn into idolatry and how crucial it is for God's servants to stay humble when people start to praise them.

God often uses success to test the heart as much as He uses suffering. When others celebrate our work or speak well of us, humility keeps us humble. Paul and Barnabas knew that every miracle and soul saved belonged to God's power, not theirs. They didn't seek applause; they sought obedience.

The Spirit empowers us to face both hardship and honor. Pride can ruin ministry as easily as persecution. When God blesses our efforts, we should, like Paul and Barnabas, keep our focus upward—away from ourselves and back to the Lord who deserves all glory.

Equipped to Persevere Through Suffering (14:19–28)

Just as the crowd in Lystra was ready to worship Paul and Barnabas, enemies from Antioch and Iconium arrived and quickly turned that same crowd against them. Human admiration can shift to hostility very fast. The people who had once shouted praises now picked up stones. They dragged Paul out of the city, assuming he was dead.

This was one of the darkest and most painful moments of Paul's ministry. Yet it also revealed the depth of his faith. Luke tells us that, *after the disciples gathered around him, he got up and went into the town.* (v. 20) The very place where he had been stoned became the place where he rose again to continue the work. There's no record of complaint or self-pity, just quiet determination. God was not finished with him yet.

The next day, Paul and Barnabas went to Derbe and made many disciples. But what stands out most is what they did afterward. Instead of taking the easy route home, they retraced their steps, going back to Lystra, Iconium, and Antioch, the same cities where they had faced violence and rejection. Their goal was not survival but strengthening. They returned to encourage the new Christians, *strengthening the disciples and encouraging them to continue in the faith.* (v. 22).

Their message was clear and honest: *It is necessary to go through many hardships to enter the kingdom of God.* They didn't sugarcoat the cost of discipleship. Following Christ involves trials, but those trials produce endurance and maturity.

Before leaving, Paul and Barnabas appointed elders in every church, prayed with fasting, and commended them to the Lord. The young congregations would need strong leadership and deep trust in God to endure. Finally, the missionaries returned to Antioch, the church that had sent them out, and reported all that God had done. Despite persecution, the mission had succeeded; new churches were planted, and the gospel had taken root.

Suffering is never wasted when it is endured for Christ. The same Spirit who called and sent Paul also strengthened him to rise again, to return, and to keep going. Every hardship became part of his equipping. God still works that way today, teaching His servants to trust Him more deeply through trials so they can strengthen others in faith.

Lesson Summary and Reflection

Key Truths from Lystra:

- God often uses hardship to equip and mature His servants.
- Courage in opposition comes from confidence in God's word and presence.
- Humility in success protects the heart and keeps glory where it belongs—with God.
- Perseverance through suffering strengthens faith and encourages others.
- The path of discipleship includes hardship, but every trial can become a testimony of God's grace.

Acts 14 reminds us that God's servants are not exempt from suffering; they are shaped by it. Paul and Barnabas encountered opposition, misunderstanding, violence, and fatigue, yet they persisted in proclaiming Christ. Whether driven out of towns or welcomed by new believers, they viewed every situation as part of God's plan.

In Iconium, they learned to stand firm in opposition. In Lystra, they learned humility in success. In Derbe and on their return trip, they learned endurance through suffering. Each trial became a tool in God's hands, equipping them to lead with deeper faith and greater compassion.

The main message in this passage is captured in Paul's words: *it is necessary to face many hardships to enter the kingdom of God.* (v. 22). Hardship is not punishment; it is preparation. God uses difficulty to strengthen His people and to demonstrate the value of the gospel to a watching world.

As Christians today, we need the same endurance. Faith that costs nothing achieves little. But when we cling to Christ through pain, rejection, or loss, our testimony becomes brighter. God never wastes suffering. Every trial teaches us trust, and every scar tells a story of His sustaining grace.

Memory Verse and Weekly Challenge

It is necessary to go through many hardships to enter the kingdom of God.
Acts 14:22 (CSB)

Weekly Challenge: When you face difficulty this week, pause and pray, "Lord, use this to strengthen my faith." Think of one person who may be struggling and share with them how God has helped you endure. Your story may give them courage to keep going.

For Discussion

1. How did Paul and Barnabas show faithfulness when they faced opposition in Iconium?

   _____

   _____

   _____

2. What can we learn from their reaction when the people of Lystra tried to worship them as gods?

   _____

   _____

   _____

3. How does Paul's response to being stoned and left for dead reveal the strength of his faith?

   _____

   _____

   _____

4. What does Acts 14:22 teach us about the role of suffering in the Christian life?

   _____

   _____

   _____

5. How can your experiences of hardship or disappointment become opportunities to strengthen others in faith?

   _____

   _____

   _____

Equipping Leaders:
The Jerusalem Council
Acts 15

*So they were sent off and went down to Antioch, and after gathering the
assembly, they delivered the letter. When they read it, they rejoiced because of
its encouragement. Both Judas and Silas, who were also prophets themselves,
encouraged the brothers and sisters and strengthened them with a long
message. After spending some time there, they were sent back in peace by the
brothers and sisters to those who had sent them. But Paul and Barnabas,
along with many others, remained in Antioch, teaching and proclaiming the
word of the Lord.*

(Acts 15:30–35)

Class Overview: Acts 15 highlights a crucial moment in the early
church—the Jerusalem Council. As the gospel spread among the
Gentiles, a heated debate arose over whether they needed to follow
the law of Moses to be saved. The apostles and elders gathered to seek
God's guidance and preserve unity within the church. Through attentive
listening, scriptural reasoning, and the leading of the Holy Spirit, they
arrived at a conclusion that affirmed salvation by grace through faith and
emphasized fellowship across cultural boundaries. This lesson shows
how godly leadership prepares the church to handle conflicts wisely,
protect the truth of the gospel, and promote peace among believers.

Class Objectives: By the end of this class, you should be able to—

1. Describe the issue that caused the dispute and why it threatened the
   unity of the early church.
2. Explain how the apostles and elders sought wisdom through
   discussion, Scripture, and the Spirit's guidance.
3. Understand that church leadership exists to protect both sound
   doctrine and loving fellowship.

4. Recognize how humility, patience, and cooperation are essential in resolving conflict.
5. Apply these principles by seeking God's wisdom and unity whenever disagreements arise in the church today.

Introduction

THE CHURCH GREW RAPIDLY, with new believers coming to Christ from all backgrounds: Jewish and Gentile, slave and free, rich and poor. However, growth raised questions. In Antioch, some Jewish Christians started teaching that Gentiles needed to be circumcised and follow the law of Moses to be saved. Their teachings challenged the core of the gospel, leading to deep division. If salvation depended on law-keeping, then grace was no longer truly grace.

The disagreement became so intense that Paul and Barnabas were sent to Jerusalem to consult the apostles and elders. What occurred there served as a model for how the church should handle conflict: with prayer, humility, Scripture, and respect for one another. Leaders did not ignore the issue or resort to anger; they listened carefully, examined what God had done among the Gentiles, and sought the Spirit's guidance together.

Through Peter's testimony, Paul and Barnabas's report, and James's wisdom from Scripture, the church recognized the truth: salvation is by grace through faith. They wrote a letter affirming unity and encouraging believers to live in peace. The Jerusalem Council settled a vital question, not by human opinion, but by divine guidance.

This moment reminds us that God equips leaders not only to teach truth but also to protect it. Conflict in the church is unavoidable, but how we handle it shows whether we trust God's wisdom or our own. Unity isn't maintained by silence or compromise; it's built when godly people seek truth together under the Spirit's guidance.

Historical Background

By the time of Acts 15, the gospel had spread well beyond Jerusalem. Through Paul and Barnabas's efforts, entire Gentile communities in Antioch, Pisidia, and Galatia embraced faith. However, not everyone in the early church understood how Gentiles fit into God's plan. Some Jewish Christians, often called "Judaizers," taught that Gentiles needed to be circumcised and obey the law of Moses to be accepted by God. They viewed Christianity as an extension of Judaism rather than as its fulfillment.

This teaching caused a serious problem. It challenged whether salvation was by grace through faith in Christ or by law-keeping and human effort. The issue was significant. It threatened the very foundation of the gospel and the unity of the church. The church in Antioch, where Jews and Gentiles worshiped together, became the center of this controversy. When the dispute couldn't be resolved locally, the congregation sent Paul, Barnabas, and others to Jerusalem to meet with the apostles and elders. This gathering—commonly called the Jerusalem Council—was the first recorded meeting of church leaders to discuss doctrine and unity.

At the council, Peter reminded everyone of his previous experience with Cornelius, demonstrating that God had already accepted Gentiles by giving them the Holy Spirit outside of the law (Acts 10–11). Paul and Barnabas shared testimony about the miracles God performed among the Gentiles during their missionary journey. Then James, the brother of Jesus, summarized the issue from Scripture, quoting Amos 9 to show that God's plan had always been to include the Gentiles as His people.

The final decision was clear: salvation comes through grace, not law. The council sent a letter confirming that Gentile believers are full members of God's family without circumcision. They only requested that believers avoid certain practices that might offend their Jewish brothers and sisters: guidelines for unity, not requirements for salvation.

The Jerusalem Council served as a model for church leadership. It demonstrated the importance of addressing conflicts through prayer, humility, and reliance on the Spirit's guidance. It also conveyed a lasting truth: no one is saved by rituals, rules, or heritage; only through the grace of the Lord Jesus Christ.

Equipped to Guard the Gospel
(15:1–6)

The opening verses of Acts 15 show how easily the gospel can be challenged when human tradition starts to replace divine truth. Some men came from Judea to Antioch teaching, *"Unless you are circumcised according to the custom prescribed by Moses, you cannot be saved."* (v. 1). To them, faith in Jesus was not enough; they wanted to add requirements that God never gave.

Paul and Barnabas quickly recognized the danger. This wasn't a small disagreement; it was an attack on the message of salvation by grace through faith. If circumcision was necessary for salvation, then the cross wasn't enough. The argument struck at the core of what it means to be saved.

Luke says, *After Paul and Barnabas had engaged them in serious argument and debate, Paul and Barnabas and some others were appointed to go up to the apostles and elders in Jerusalem about this issue.* (v. 2). Notice the humility and order in their response. They didn't divide the church or rely on emotion. They sought the collective wisdom of godly leaders. They wanted to ensure the gospel was preserved for every brother and sister. As they traveled to Jerusalem, they passed through Phoenicia and Samaria, sharing the good news of Gentile conversions, which brought joy to all the believers. Even amid controversy, they kept the focus on what God was doing.

Here we learn an essential lesson about leadership: God equips His servants to guard the gospel. Every generation faces pressures to add, change, or distort the message of grace. Faithful leaders must know Scripture well enough to recognize error and courageous enough to confront it in love. Guarding the gospel requires both conviction and humility, conviction to stand for truth, and humility to seek unity under God's word. The early church didn't settle for compromise or confusion; they came together to protect the good news that Jesus alone saves. That same task still belongs to us today.

Equipped to Seek God's Wisdom
(15:7–21)

When the church in Jerusalem gathered to address the dispute, there was "much debate." This wasn't a quick or easy discussion. Faithful men wrestled with a difficult question that affected the future of the church. Yet what stands out is how the leaders sought God's wisdom together. They didn't let emotion or pride control the conversation. They listened, they reasoned from Scripture, and they watched for the Spirit's direction.

Peter was the first to speak. He reminded the assembly of what God had already done through him years earlier when he preached to Cornelius and his household (Acts 10–11). The Holy Spirit had come upon them without circumcision or observing the law. Peter concluded, *now then, why are you testing God by putting a yoke on the disciples' necks that neither our ancestors nor we have been able to bear? On the contrary, we believe that we are saved through the grace of the Lord Jesus in the same way they are.* (vv. 10–11).

Next, Paul and Barnabas described how God had worked signs and wonders among the Gentiles on their missionary journey. Their testimony confirmed Peter's point: God Himself had accepted the Gentiles by faith, not by law.

Then James, the brother of Jesus, stood to speak. As a respected leader in the Jerusalem church, his words carried weight. He pointed to Scripture, quoting from Amos 9, to show that God had always planned to include the Gentiles in His people. He proposed a wise and balanced solution: do not burden Gentile believers with the law of Moses but ask them to abstain from certain practices that would unnecessarily offend Jewish believers. This was not law-keeping for salvation, but wisdom for fellowship.

Here we see a glimpse of what Spirit-led leadership looks like. The apostles didn't rely on opinion or politics; they sought the Lord's will through His Word and His work. They listened to testimony, weighed evidence, and reasoned from Scripture. The result was not division but clarity and peace.

When God's people face disagreement, this passage gives us a model to follow. We must slow down, pray, listen, and let the Spirit speak through His word. Wisdom is not found in winning arguments but in aligning hearts with God's revealed truth.

Equipped to Preserve Unity (15:22–35)

After prayer, testimony, and agreement, the apostles and elders reached a unified decision. They decided to send a letter to the Gentile Christians, along with trusted men, Judas (called Barsabbas) and Silas, to deliver the message. The church wanted to ensure the news came not from hearsay but from the very leaders who had prayed and discussed together.

The letter began with encouragement, not condemnation: *Since we have heard that some without our authorization went out from us and troubled you with their words... we have unanimously decided to select men and send them to you.* (vv. 24–25). The decision was presented as a shared conviction under divine guidance: *For it was the Holy Spirit's decision— and ours—not to place further burdens on you beyond these requirements.* (v. 28).

The message reaffirmed the core of the gospel: salvation is by grace through faith. The few instructions given, abstaining from food offered to idols, from blood, from things strangled, and from sexual immorality, were not conditions for salvation but acts of love. These guidelines helped promote unity between Jewish and Gentile believers, allowing them to share fellowship without causing offense.

When the letter arrived in Antioch, the church celebrated. The message provided reassurance and motivation, strengthening the believers and bringing peace. Silas and Judas, both prophets, stayed for a while to teach and uplift. The conflict that once threatened to divide the church now became a chance for better understanding and unity.

God equips leaders not only to teach truth but also to foster peace. Unity doesn't mean everyone agrees on every detail; it means the church is connected through shared faith in Jesus Christ and submission to the

Spirit's will. Leaders maintain unity by listening carefully, speaking honestly, and acting with humility and love.

In a time where division comes easily, the Jerusalem Council stands as a model for the modern church. When we face disagreement, we must hold tightly to the essentials of faith and treat one another with patience and grace. The Spirit who guided those leaders in Jerusalem still leads the church today when we seek Him together.

Lesson Summary and Reflection

Key Truths about the Jerusalem Council:

- God equips leaders to protect both the truth of the gospel and the unity of the church.
- Salvation is by grace through faith in Jesus Christ: never by law, ritual, or heritage.
- The Holy Spirit provides wisdom when we seek God's will together in humility.
- True unity is built on shared faith, patient listening, and mutual love.
- Wise leadership turns conflict into an opportunity for growth and greater understanding.

The Jerusalem Council was a defining moment for the early church. Faced with division over the law of Moses and salvation, the apostles and elders gathered to listen, pray, and seek the Spirit's guidance. The outcome preserved both the truth of the gospel and the unity of the body.

The leaders did not settle the issue through pride or pressure but through patient dialogue and submission to God's word. Peter reminded them that salvation is by grace through faith. Paul and Barnabas testified to God's work among the Gentiles. James confirmed their testimony with Scripture, showing that God had always planned to include all nations in His people. Together they affirmed that faith, not ritual, makes a person right with God.

The council's letter to the Gentile believers reflected humility and care. Rather than impose burdens, they encouraged practices that would promote peace and fellowship. The church rejoiced because truth and love had prevailed.

God equips leaders to protect doctrine and lead people toward unity. The health of a congregation depends not only on what is taught but also on how conflicts are managed. When we seek God's wisdom together, through prayer, Scripture, and humility, the Spirit guides us to peace. Leaders who follow this pattern build churches that are strong in truth, gentle in spirit, and united in love.

Memory Verse and Weekly Challenge

We believe that we are saved through the grace of the Lord Jesus in the same way they are.

Acts 15:11 (CSB)

Weekly Challenge: This week, pray for wisdom and humility in how you handle disagreement: at home, at work, or in the church. When differences arise, listen before speaking and seek what will build peace and truth. Ask God to make you a source of unity, not division, in His family.

For Discussion

1. Why was the question raised in Acts 15 such a serious threat to the gospel and the unity of the church?

   _____

   _____

   _____

2. How did the apostles and elders show humility and dependence on God's word in handling the dispute?

   _____

   _____

   _____

3. What can modern church leaders learn from the way Peter, Paul, Barnabas, and James worked together?

   _____

   _____

   _____

4. How does Acts 15 remind us that unity must be built on truth, not compromise?

_____

_____

_____

5. In what ways can you personally contribute to unity and peace in your congregation this week?

_____

_____

_____

Equipped for New Opportunities: The Macedonian Call

Acts 16:6–15

During the night Paul had a vision in which a Macedonian man was standing and pleading with him, "Cross over to Macedonia and help us!"
Acts 16:9

Class Overview: Acts 16 marks a turning point in the spread of the gospel. For the first time, the message of Christ crossed into Europe, beginning a new chapter in God's mission. As Paul and his companions traveled through Asia Minor, the Holy Spirit repeatedly redirected their plans. Then, through a vision in the night, God called them to Macedonia. This lesson shows how God opens new doors, guides His servants in unexpected ways, and equips believers to seize opportunities for His glory. From divine direction to the conversion of Lydia in Philippi, we see how God's Spirit leads and blesses those who are willing to follow His call.

Class Objectives: By the end of this class, you should be able to—

1. Explain how the Holy Spirit redirected Paul's missionary journey and opened new opportunities in Macedonia.
2. Recognize the importance of sensitivity to God's leading when plans change.
3. Describe the conversion of Lydia and its significance in the spread of the gospel into Europe.
4. Understand how obedience in small steps prepares believers for greater mission work.
5. Apply the lesson by learning to trust God's guidance and look for open doors to serve Him daily.

Introduction

EVERY CHRISTIAN EVENTUALLY LEARNS THAT GOD'S PLANS often look different from our own. Paul had a clear idea of where he wanted to go next in his mission work, but the Lord had another direction in mind. As Acts 16 opens, Paul and his team, Silas, Timothy, and soon Luke, were traveling through Asia Minor, preaching and strengthening churches. Their hearts were eager, but each time they tried to move forward, the Holy Spirit stopped them. They were forbidden to speak in certain regions and prevented from going where they planned.

Then, in the quiet of the night, God gave Paul a vision: a man from Macedonia pleading, *"Come over and help us."* That single vision changed the course of history. For the first time, the gospel would spread into Europe—into places like Philippi, Thessalonica, and Corinth. God was opening a new frontier for the message of Christ.

The lesson from this passage is clear: divine interruptions are often divine invitations. Paul's closed doors were not failures; they were guidance. When one path ended, God was steering him toward a greater opportunity. The same is true for us. God may redirect our plans to position us where He can use us most effectively.

When Paul obeyed the vision, he and his companions immediately set sail for Macedonia. In Philippi, the district's leading city, they met Lydia, a woman whose heart the Lord opened to respond to the message. Through her conversion, the first church in Europe was born. Acts 16 reminds us that God's mission always moves forward, but not always on our timetable. The Spirit equips us not only to serve but also to listen, to wait, and to follow when the next open door appears.

Historical Background

The events in Acts 16 take place during Paul's second missionary journey, roughly A.D. 49–52. After the Jerusalem Council decided on the issue of Gentile inclusion (Acts 15), Paul set out once again to strengthen the churches he had established during his first trip. He traveled with Silas and later brought Timothy along to Lystra, where he was a young disciple respected by the local believers. Luke, the author of Acts, joined them soon afterward, which is clear from the shift in the narrative to "we" in verse 10.

Their plan was to move westward through the regions of Phrygia and Galatia, then into the province of Asia (modern western Turkey). However, the Holy Spirit "forbade" them to speak the word there. They next tried to go north into Bithynia, but "the Spirit of Jesus did not allow them." With their paths blocked, the missionaries traveled to Troas, a port city on the Aegean Sea near ancient Troy.

It was there that God revealed the next step: a vision of a man from Macedonia pleading for help. Macedonia was a region across the sea in northern Greece, part of Europe. Cities like Philippi, Thessalonica, and Berea lay ahead—places that would become key centers of Christian faith. Paul's immediate obedience to the vision showed his trust in God's guidance.

When Paul and his team arrived in Philippi, they entered a prominent Roman colony known for its military veterans and Roman pride. Since there was no synagogue, they went to a place of prayer by the river, where they met Lydia, a merchant from Thyatira who sold purple cloth. She was a worshiper of God, open and sincere. The Lord opened her heart to accept Paul's message, and she and her household were baptized. Her home soon became the meeting place of the first church in Europe.

The gospel's movement into Europe fulfilled God's promise that His salvation would reach the ends of the earth. Through the Spirit's redirection, Paul learned that closed doors often lead to greater opportunities and that God's plan is always larger than our own vision.

Equipped to Follow God's Direction (16:6–10)

Paul and his companions had a plan. They wanted to keep preaching throughout Asia, where major cities like Ephesus offered great potential for the gospel. However, as they moved forward, the Holy Spirit repeatedly prevented them. Luke says they were "forbidden by the Holy Spirit to speak the word in Asia" (v. 6) and later that "the Spirit of Jesus did not allow them" (v. 7). No explanation is given—only that God closed the door.

For men with missionary zeal, that must have been frustrating. But the Spirit was not hindering the gospel; He was guiding it. Sometimes God says "no" because He is preparing a better "yes." The missionaries obeyed, even when they didn't understand. Instead of forcing their plans, they followed the Spirit's lead until they reached Troas—a coastal city where God would make His will clear.

That night, Paul had a vision of a man from Macedonia pleading, *'Come over to Macedonia and help us!'* When Paul shared the vision, the team immediately concluded that "God had called us to preach the gospel to them." (v. 10). They didn't delay or debate. They trusted that the same Spirit who closed doors had now opened one.

This short passage shares an important truth about God's guidance: the Spirit equips us not just to act, but also to wait. Obedience sometimes involves pausing as much as moving forward. Closed doors can be painful, but they shield us from paths that aren't part of God's plan. The key is staying sensitive to the Spirit's leading and being ready to move when He calls.

Following God's guidance requires humility. We often desire control, but the Spirit shapes us through surrender. When Paul and his companions set aside their own plans, they found themselves at the heart of God's plan to bring the gospel into Europe for the first time.

Equipped to Seize God's Opportunities (16:11–13)

When Paul and his team understood God's call, they acted without hesitation. Luke writes, *"From Troas we put out to sea and sailed straight for Samothrace, the next day to Neapolis, and from there to Philippi"* (v. 11–12). The phrase "straight for" suggests favorable winds and eager hearts. Obedience to God's direction brought clarity and momentum.

Philippi was a Roman colony and the main city of Macedonia. Its citizens took pride in their Roman identity, and the city showcased Rome's culture and privileges. Paul and his companions found themselves in completely new territory: unfamiliar people, new customs, and no synagogue to start with. Still, they trusted that God had brought them there for a purpose.

On the Sabbath, they went outside the city gate to the river, where they expected to find a place of prayer. This small act of faith showed their readiness to seize any opportunity God provided. There may have been only a few worshipers, mostly women, but that was enough for God to begin His work. The apostles didn't wait for a crowd or perfect conditions. They shared the message wherever they went, with those willing to listen.

Divine opportunities often start small. The first church in Europe did not begin in a grand synagogue or public forum but beside a river, with a few sincere seekers. When God opens a door, it might not look impressive, but obedience turns small beginnings into eternal impact.

The Spirit equips us not only to discern God's call but also to respond to it immediately. Like Paul, we must learn to move when God says move; to see every person, every moment, and every open door as opportunities to serve His purpose.

Equipped to Witness God's Power (16:14–15)

Among the women gathered at the river that day was Lydia, a merchant from the city of Thyatira. She sold purple cloth, a luxury fabric worn by the wealthy and powerful, indicating that she was a woman of means and influence. Luke describes her as "a worshiper of God," meaning she believed in the God of Israel but had not yet heard the gospel of Christ.

As Paul spoke, something remarkable happened. *The Lord opened her heart to respond to what Paul was saying.* (v. 14) That simple phrase captures the essence of all true conversion. The power to believe does not come from persuasion or emotion but from God working through His Word. Lydia's open heart was the work of God. The Spirit who had directed Paul to Macedonia now opened her soul to salvation.

Lydia believed and was baptized, along with her household. Her immediate obedience demonstrates a genuine and living faith. Then, out of gratitude, she invited Paul and his companions to stay in her home, saying, *"If you consider me a believer in the Lord, come and stay at my house."* (v. 15) Her home soon became the first meeting place of the Philippian church, serving as a base for gospel work throughout Europe.

Here we witness the quiet strength of God's providence. Paul followed the Spirit's guidance, and God arranged everything: an open heart, a receptive listener, and a new beginning for the gospel in a new land. Lydia's story reminds us that no place is too distant, and no person is too unlikely, for God to reach.

The Spirit equips us not only to preach but also to witness—to see firsthand how God's word transforms lives. Every act of obedience creates an opportunity for God to reveal His grace. The same Spirit who guided Paul and opened Lydia's heart still works through faithful followers today, one conversation at a time.

Lesson Summary and Reflection

Key Truths from Philippi:

- God sometimes closes doors to guide His people toward better opportunities.
- The Holy Spirit equips us to listen, wait, and respond when God redirects our plans.
- Obedience, even in small steps, opens the way for God's greater work.
- True success in mission begins with open hearts, not perfect plans.
- God's power is revealed when His people follow His leading with faith and humility.

Acts 16:6–15 tells a story of divine guidance, obedience, and fresh starts. Paul and his companions realized that being led by the Spirit requires willingness to change direction. Closed doors in Asia and Bithynia were not setbacks but God's way of guiding them toward Macedonia, where a new mission field was waiting. When they followed God's lead, they became part of His plan to bring the gospel to Europe.

God's work often begins quietly. A prayer meeting by a river became the birthplace of a new church. Lydia's open-hearted response and faithfulness show that the mission's success didn't rely on numbers or strategy but on the power of God's word.

We need to learn to hold our plans loosely and our faith tightly. God equips His people not just to speak but to listen, to recognize when He is guiding us differently, and to step forward when He opens the way. Each of us encounters crossroads where obedience calls for trust. When we walk through the doors God opens, we can be confident His grace will meet us there, and His purpose will continue.

Memory Verse and Weekly Challenge

During the night Paul had a vision in which a Macedonian man was standing and pleading with him, "Cross over to Macedonia and help us!"
Acts 16:9 (CSB)

Weekly Challenge: Think of a time when God closed one door and opened another. How did that shape your faith? This week, pray for eyes to see new opportunities the Lord may be placing before you. Be willing to act when He calls, even if it leads you somewhere unexpected.

For Discussion

1. What does Acts 16 teach you about how God guides His people?

   _____

   _____

   _____

2. How do you usually respond when your plans are interrupted or redirected?

   _____

   _____

   _____

3. What can we learn from Paul's immediate obedience to the vision from Macedonia?

   _____

   _____

   _____

4. How does Lydia's conversion show the quiet power of God's word at work?

_____

_____

_____

5. Where might God be calling you to step forward in faith right now—to serve, to speak, or to trust Him in a new way?

_____

_____

_____

Equipped Through Opposition: Paul in Philippi
Acts 16:16–40

About midnight Paul and Silas were praying and singing hymns to God, and the prisoners were listening to them (Acts 16:25).

Class Overview: The ministry in Philippi started with an open heart—but quickly faced hardship. After Lydia's conversion, Paul and Silas encountered fierce opposition when they expelled a spirit from a slave girl who made her owners profit through fortune-telling. Their act of mercy resulted in arrest, beating, and imprisonment. Yet even in chains, their faith remained strong. God used their suffering to open new doors, including the conversion of the Philippian jailer and his family. This lesson teaches that opposition is not a sign of failure but often the place where God's power is most clearly seen. The Spirit equips believers to worship in suffering, trust in trials, and witness through adversity.

Class Objectives: By the end of this class, you should be able to—

1. Describe the events that led to Paul and Silas's imprisonment in Philippi.
2. Explain how their response to persecution revealed the strength of their faith.
3. Understand how God can use opposition and suffering to advance the gospel.
4. Identify the transformation seen in the Philippian jailer and what it teaches about salvation.
5. Apply these truths by choosing faith and praise in life's difficulties, trusting that God can use every circumstance for His glory.

Introduction

FAITH IS OFTEN TESTED IN DIFFICULT TIMES. In Acts 16, Paul and Silas discovered that following God's call doesn't always bring comfort. After answering the man from Macedonia's vision, they reached Philippi, where the gospel quickly took hold. Lydia and her family believed, and the first church in Europe was established. However, as soon as the work began, opposition appeared.

As they headed to the place of prayer, a slave girl possessed by a spirit began following them, shouting loudly about who they were. Although her words appeared to be true, her spirit was not. Paul finally ordered the spirit to leave her in the name of Jesus Christ—and it did. Her freedom cost her owners their income, and anger quickly turned into accusations. The city authorities sided with the crowd, and Paul and Silas were stripped, beaten, and thrown into prison.

What follows is one of the most powerful examples of faith in adversity found in Scripture. Bound in stocks, their bodies aching, Paul and Silas prayed and sang hymns to God in the middle of the night. Their songs became a testimony to every prisoner listening—and to heaven itself. Then, in a moment of divine power, an earthquake shook the prison, opening the doors and loosening every chain.

Opposition is not the end of God's work; it often serves as the means by which His glory is revealed. When believers respond to hardship with worship and trust, the world takes notice. Through pain, Paul and Silas became instruments of salvation for a Roman jailer and his family. Their story teaches us that God equips His people not only to preach freely but also to praise through suffering.

Historical Background

Philippi was one of the leading cities in Macedonia, a Roman colony settled largely by retired soldiers. Its people took great pride in their Roman citizenship and loyalty to the empire. As a result, they were often suspicious of new religious movements, especially those seen as threatening Roman order. The city's status and culture help explain why Paul and Silas faced such strong resistance.

After arriving in Philippi, Paul and his team met Lydia, whose home became their base of operations. From there, they continued sharing the gospel. But their ministry drew attention when Paul freed a slave girl possessed by a spirit of divination. The Greek word used describes a "python spirit," associated with the temple of Apollo at Delphi, a spirit believed to give prophetic power. Her owners had exploited her for profit, and when Paul cast out the demon, their financial gain vanished.

The men seized Paul and Silas, dragged them before the magistrates, and accused them of disturbing the peace and promoting unlawful customs. Their appeal to Roman pride was strategic: "These men are Jews and are advocating customs that are not lawful for us as Romans to adopt or practice." (v. 21). Without investigation or trial, the magistrates ordered Paul and Silas to be beaten with rods, a severe and humiliating punishment, and thrown into prison under strict guard.

The jailer, likely a retired soldier himself, placed them in the inner cell and fastened their feet in stocks. Yet in this place of pain and injustice, the power of God would be displayed most clearly. Around midnight, the prisoners heard hymns of praise echo through the darkness. Then, a great earthquake shook the foundations of the prison, opening every door and unfastening every chain.

Roman law held jailers personally responsible for the lives of their prisoners. Fearing execution, the jailer prepared to take his own life, but Paul's voice stopped him. What followed was one of the most beautiful scenes in Acts: the jailer fell before Paul and Silas and asked, "Sirs, what must I do to be saved?" (v. 30). That night, he and his whole household were baptized.

The next day, when the city officials learned that Paul and Silas were Roman citizens, they realized their mistake and apologized publicly. The gospel had triumphed, and a new congregation was firmly planted in Philippi, a church that would become one of Paul's dearest partners in ministry. The kingdom of God advances not through ease, but through endurance. In every act of opposition, God was equipping His servants to trust Him more deeply and to witness to His grace more powerfully.

Equipped to Confront Evil
(16:16–21)

As Paul and his companions continued their work in Philippi, they encountered a slave girl possessed by a spirit of divination. Her owners exploited her to tell fortunes, earning a lot of money from her condition. Day after day, she followed Paul and Silas, crying out, *these men are proclaiming to you the way of salvation.* Her words were technically true, but her spirit was not from God. Evil often hides within partial truths.

Paul endured this for several days until, filled with the Spirit, he turned and said to the spirit, *I command you in the name of Jesus Christ to come out of her!* Immediately, the girl was freed. One act of spiritual authority broke years of oppression. The gospel not only saved a soul but also challenged a system of exploitation.

But freedom for one meant anger for others. Her owners, now deprived of their income, seized Paul and Silas and dragged them before the city magistrates. They stirred the crowd with false accusations, saying, *these men are Jews and are advocating customs that are not lawful for us as Romans to adopt or practice.* (v. 21). Prejudice and greed combined to ignite public outrage.

This episode demonstrates that the gospel consistently challenges evil, whether it exists in individuals or society. As the kingdom of God advances, it threatens those who profit from sin and injustice. That's why opposition often follows obedience. The Spirit who empowers believers to preach also empowers them to confront darkness with courage.

Paul didn't seek confrontation, but he didn't avoid it either. Evil must be exposed so that true freedom can come. The church today must remember that spiritual warfare is real and that silence in the face of evil is not an option. We are called to speak truth in love, trusting that Christ's authority is greater than the world's hostility.

Equipped to Worship in Suffering
(16:22–26)

The crowd in Philippi became violent. Without a trial or defense, Paul and Silas were stripped, beaten with rods, and thrown into prison. The magistrates ordered the jailer to keep them under close watch. He put them in the innermost cell, the darkest and most secure part of the prison, and fastened their feet in stocks. Their backs were bruised and bleeding. They were physically and emotionally drained.

What happened next defies explanation except for faith. *Around midnight, Paul and Silas were praying and singing hymns to God, and the prisoners were listening to them* (v. 25). In their pain, they chose praise. Instead of questioning God, they worshiped Him. Their joy did not depend on circumstances—it flowed from trust in His presence.

One of the deepest truths about the Christian life is that worship is most powerful when it comes from the valley. Paul and Silas were obedient, yet they suffered unjustly. Still, they understood that their chains could not silence the gospel. Their song in the night became a testament to everyone around them— the prisoners who listened, the jailer who watched, and the God who heard.

Then God moved. A violent earthquake shook the prison, opening all the doors and loosening every chain. Yet no one escaped. The miracle was not just in the shaking of the ground but in the peace that kept everyone still. God was showing that His power is greater than any prison and His presence deeper than any pain.

Worship in suffering does more than comfort us; it shows the world that God is worthy of praise even when life hurts. It is the clearest expression of faith and the strongest form of witness. The Spirit equips believers to sing through the pain, to trust through the tears, and to find in every trial an opportunity to glorify God.

Equipped to Witness Through Adversity
(16:27–40)

When the earthquake struck and the prison doors flew open, the jailer awoke in terror. Under Roman law, a guard who lost his prisoners could be executed. Believing everyone had escaped, he drew his sword to take his own life. But Paul's voice stopped him: *Don't harm yourself, because we're all here!* (v. 28).

That cry of compassion changed everything. The man who had locked Paul and Silas in chains suddenly found himself trembling before them, asking, *Sirs, what must I do to be saved?* (v. 30). Their answer was simple and timeless: *Believe in the Lord Jesus, and you will be saved—you and your household.* (v. 31). The gospel Paul had preached in synagogues and marketplaces was now proclaimed in a prison cell.

That same night, the jailer cleaned their wounds, a sign of repentance and compassion, and he and his entire family were baptized. Joy filled his house as he prepared a meal for the men he had once guarded. This is the transforming power of grace: enemies become brothers, wounds become testimony, and suffering becomes the doorway to salvation.

The next morning, the magistrates ordered Paul and Silas to be released quietly. But Paul refused to leave silently. As a Roman citizen, he had been beaten and imprisoned unlawfully. He insisted that the officials come and release them publicly. His goal was not revenge but protection; he wanted the new Philippian church to be free from suspicion or fear. The magistrates apologized for their mistake and asked Paul and Silas to leave the city.

Before leaving, they went back to Lydia's house to encourage the believers. The same city that had once beaten them now had a growing church, including a businesswoman, a former slave girl, and a Roman jailer. Opposition had not stopped the gospel; it had made it grow more. Through hardships, God prepared His servants to witness His power. Every setback became a chance for grace. Every wound was a doorway to salvation's message. The Spirit still uses suffering today, turning difficulty into testimony and pain into praise.

Lesson Summary and Reflection

Key Truths from a Philippi:

- The gospel confronts evil and exposes systems that profit from sin.
- God's servants can worship even in suffering because His presence never leaves them.
- True faith shines brightest when tested by opposition.
- God turns hardship into opportunity and pain into a powerful witness.
- The Spirit equips us to respond to adversity with grace, courage, and praise.

God's power often shines brightest in the darkest places. Their obedience to the Macedonian call did not lead to comfort but to conflict. Yet, through that opposition, God revealed His strength and grace in unforgettable ways.

They confronted evil by freeing a young slave girl from spiritual bondage, demonstrating that the gospel liberates both body and soul. They endured injustice and pain without bitterness, showing that worship can rise even from a prison cell. And they witnessed powerfully through adversity, leading a hardened Roman jailer and his family to salvation.

What the enemy intended to harm, God turned into an opportunity. The prison became a place of praise. Suffering became the platform for evangelism. The beating that should have silenced them turned into the spark that birthed the Philippian church. Faith isn't about comfort but about courage. The Spirit equips us not just to resist evil but to sing through suffering and shine in adversity. When life feels unfair or heavy, remember that God's power isn't absent; it's often preparing to do its greatest work.

Memory Verse and Weekly Challenge

About midnight Paul and Silas were praying and singing hymns to God,
and the prisoners were listening to them.
Acts 16:25 (CSB)

Weekly Challenge: Choose worship over worry. When you face
pressure, disappointment, or conflict, stop and pray as Paul and Silas did.
Sing, give thanks, or read Scripture aloud. Then look for how God might
use your response to encourage someone else who's watching your faith.

For Discussion

1. What does the story of the slave girl reveal about how the gospel
   confronts evil in the world?

   _____

   _____

2. How did Paul and Silas's response to suffering set them apart from
   the crowd around them?

   _____

   _____

3. What can we learn from their midnight prayers and songs about
   trusting God in hardship?

   _____

   _____

4. How does the conversion of the Philippian jailer show God's ability
   to bring good out of adversity?

   _____

   _____

5. When you face opposition or difficulty, how can your faith and
   response become a testimony to others?

   _____

   _____

   _____

Equipped to Engage Culture: Paul in Athens

Acts 17:16–34

For as I was passing through and observing the objects of your worship, I even found an altar on which was inscribed: To an Unknown God. Therefore, what you worship in ignorance, this I proclaim to you.
Acts 17:23

Class Overview: When Paul arrived in Athens, he entered a city known for its philosophy, art, and education, but also for its idolatry. Surrounded by altars, temples, and endless debates, Paul's spirit was troubled. Yet instead of withdrawing, he engaged the culture with wisdom, courage, and grace. In this passage, Paul demonstrates how to share the truth in a skeptical world—starting where people are, affirming what is true, and then pointing them to the God they do not yet know. This lesson emphasizes that the Spirit equips believers to communicate the gospel clearly in every setting, using discernment, compassion, and conviction to reach hearts influenced by the world.

Class Objectives: By the end of this class, you should be able to—

1. Describe the spiritual and cultural atmosphere of ancient Athens and how it mirrors today's world.
2. Understand how Paul built bridges between biblical truth and Athenian beliefs.
3. Recognize that effective evangelism requires both courage and compassion.
4. Identify key truths Paul used to explain the nature of God and the resurrection of Christ.
5. Apply Paul's example by learning to share faith thoughtfully and respectfully with those shaped by modern culture.

Introduction

ATHENS WAS THE INTELLECTUAL HEART OF THE ANCIENT WORLD. The city had been home to philosophers like Socrates, Plato, and Aristotle. Its streets were filled with sculptures, temples, and monuments dedicated to Greek gods. Wherever Paul looked, he saw signs of human ingenuity and confusion. Luke writes that Paul's spirit was "deeply distressed" as he saw that the city was full of idols.

To the Athenians, religion was a topic of curiosity and discussion. They enjoyed debating new ideas but hesitated to make commitments. The Areopagus, or Mars Hill, served as the meeting place for philosophers and leaders to hear and evaluate new teachings. When Paul began preaching about Jesus and the resurrection, they invited him to speak there, not because they believed, but because they were curious.

Paul's approach in Athens differed from his sermons in the synagogues. His audience didn't know the Scriptures or share his background. Instead of quoting prophets, he began with creation. Instead of condemning their ignorance, he built a bridge from what they already understood, pointing to the altar "to an unknown god" as his starting point. From there, he revealed the true and living God who made the world, gives life to all, and now calls everyone to repent.

God will empower us to speak truth in a world shaped by culture, philosophy, and doubt. Paul's approach was not compromise; it was clarity. He met people where they were but refused to leave them there. The Spirit still urges believers to do the same: to understand the world around us, recognize its lostness, and communicate the gospel in ways that reach both the mind and the heart.

Historical Background

By the time Paul reached Athens, the city's political heyday had passed, but its role as a hub of learning and philosophy remained unmatched. Athens was the intellectual center of the Greco-Roman world: a city teeming with scholars, artists, and philosophers who influenced how people thought about truth, morality, and religion.

Although Athens is renowned for its beauty and culture, it was also highly religious. Temples dedicated to Greek gods lined nearly every street. The Parthenon, devoted to Athena, stood prominently on the Acropolis. Altars for Zeus, Apollo, Hermes, and numerous other gods could be seen throughout the city. Ancient writers said it was easier to find a god in Athens than a man.

Two main philosophical groups shaped Athenian thought:

- The Epicureans believed the gods were distant and uninterested in human affairs. They sought happiness through pleasure and freedom from pain, living by the motto, "Enjoy life now."
- The Stoics taught self-control and virtue, believing that reason governed the universe. They emphasized duty, moral discipline, and acceptance of fate.

When Paul preached about Jesus and the resurrection, both groups felt intrigued and confused. Some dismissed him as a "babbler," while others wanted to learn more. The idea of resurrection challenged everything they believed—most Greeks thought the body was a prison for the soul, not something to be raised again.

The Areopagus (or Mars Hill) was a council that gathered near the Acropolis. It served both as a court and a place for public discussion. Speaking there was considered a great honor. Paul's invitation to share his teachings before this group gave him the chance to address Athens' leading thinkers.

Paul's message challenged both idolatry and human philosophy. He declared that the one true God created the world, sustains life, rules over all nations, and will one day judge the world through the risen Christ. His sermon in Athens stands as a prime example of effectively communicating the gospel to people unfamiliar with Scripture—truth delivered with logic, respect, and conviction.

Acts 17 remains relevant today. Like Athens, our modern world values knowledge, creativity, and tolerance but often dismisses absolute truth. God still equips His people, as He did Paul, to engage culture with understanding hearts and courageous faith.

Equipped to See the World As It Is
(17:16–21)

When Paul entered Athens, he saw more than art, architecture, and philosophy; he saw lost souls. Luke writes, *"While Paul was waiting for them in Athens, he was deeply distressed when he saw that the city was full of idols"* (v. 16). The word 'distressed' describes a sharp inner stirring, a grief that comes from seeing God's glory replaced by human substitutes. Paul's reaction was not anger toward the people but sorrow for their blindness.

Everywhere he looked, religion filled the city, yet truth was missing. The Athenians were dedicated to worship, but their worship was misguided. Their temples were crowded, but their hearts remained empty. Paul's response shows what equips believers to engage culture: compassion based on truth. He didn't disdain the culture; he aimed to reach it.

Paul began sharing his reasoning in the synagogue with Jews and God-fearing Gentiles, and each day in the marketplace with anyone who was there. The marketplace (the *agora*) was the heart of daily life, a place for commerce, conversation, and philosophy. Paul took the gospel out of the building and into the streets. His faith wasn't limited to formal worship; it was relevant to everyday life.

Soon, he attracted the attention of two dominant philosophical groups: the Epicureans, who pursued pleasure and rejected divine involvement, and the Stoics, who aimed for virtue through reason and self-control. To both, Paul's message about Jesus and the resurrection sounded strange. Some mocked him, calling him a "babbler," meaning someone who sifts through scraps of ideas without understanding. Others were curious to hear more.

Paul's example shows that the first step in engaging culture is learning to see it as God does. It's easy to become numb or cynical about the world's idolatry, but Paul's heart was moved. He didn't ignore what he saw; he allowed it to motivate him to action. A church that feels nothing for a lost world will never reach it. The Spirit equips us not to condemn culture from afar but to enter it with eyes open and hearts burdened for truth.

Equipped to Build Bridges of Truth
(17:22–29)

Standing before the council of the Areopagus, Paul delivered one of the most thoughtful and powerful messages ever recorded in Scripture. He addressed men of learning, influence, and pride. Yet he didn't start with attack or accusation. Instead, he showed respect: *"People of Athens, I see that you are extremely religious in every respect."* (v. 22). He recognized their search for meaning—a pursuit that, though misguided, revealed a spiritual hunger.

Paul then pointed to what they already knew but didn't understand: an altar inscribed *"To an Unknown God."* This was his starting point: a bridge from their confusion to the truth. "What you worship in ignorance," he said, "this I proclaim to you." Paul didn't change the message; he changed the approach. He began where they were and led them to who God is.

He described God as the Creator, meaning the One who made the world and everything in it (v. 24). He is the Lord of heaven and earth, not limited to temples built by human hands. He is the Giver of life, not dependent on human offerings. And He is Sovereign, setting the times and borders of nations so that people might seek Him and find Him (vv. 26–27).

Then Paul condemned the emptiness of idolatry: *We shouldn't think that the divine nature is like gold, silver, or stone—an image shaped by human art and imagination.* (v. 29). Humanity cannot create God; God created humanity. By quoting their own poets: "For we are also his offspring," Paul demonstrated that truth is universal because it comes from the same Creator.

This moment shows how we can engage with the world without sacrificing truth. Paul didn't dilute the gospel, but he spoke in a way the Athenians could understand. He built bridges with wisdom and grace. His goal wasn't to win an argument but to reveal the living God behind their empty religion.

God continues to equip His followers today. We live in a world filled with competing ideas and man-made idols, such as success, self, pleasure, and pride. Our task is to start where people are and gently guide them toward the truth they already sense but have not fully grasped. The Spirit gives us both the courage to speak and the discernment to relate truth to real life.

Equipped to Call the World to Repentance (17:30–34)

After establishing common ground, Paul addressed the core of his message. He stated, *Therefore, having overlooked the times of ignorance, God now commands all people everywhere to repent.* (v. 30). The era of speculation and superstition was finished. God revealed Himself through His Son, and every individual is responsible for responding.

Paul's audience valued knowledge and debate, but he spoke with authority, not just theory. The call to repentance was not optional; it was urgent. The reason was clear: *God has set a day when he will judge the world in righteousness by the man he has appointed. He has provided proof of this to everyone by raising him from the dead.* (v. 31)

The resurrection was Paul's dividing line. It declared that Jesus was more than a moral teacher or a noble martyr. He was the living Lord who conquered death. For Greek thinkers who viewed the body as a prison, the idea of bodily resurrection was offensive and absurd. Some mocked openly. Others said they would hear him again later. Yet a few believed, including Dionysius, a member of the Areopagus, and a woman named Damaris.

Paul's message reminds us that engaging with culture always leads to a moment of decision. Some will laugh, some will hesitate, and some will believe. Our task is not to control the response but to faithfully declare the truth. The Spirit equips us to speak clearly, love deeply, and trust that God will open the hearts He chooses.

The call to repentance remains unchanged. The world still worships idols of intellect, pleasure, or power, but the gospel still proclaims: the true and living God calls everyone to turn from sin and trust in the risen Christ. Like Paul, we must proclaim that message with both courage and compassion, knowing that eternity hangs in the balance.

Lesson Summary and Reflection

Key Truths from Athens:

- The Spirit equips us to see the world's idolatry with compassion, not contempt.
- Effective evangelism begins where people are and leads them to who God is.
- The gospel must be spoken with both truth and grace: never watered down, never harsh.
- God calls all people everywhere to repent and believe in the risen Christ.
- Faithful witness means trusting God with the results, even when the world mocks or resists.

Paul's visit to Athens is a prime example of how to share the gospel in a world influenced by culture, intellect, and confusion. He didn't approach the Athenians with hostility or fear but with conviction and compassion. Their idolatry moved his heart, his mind was prepared with truth, and his words were guided by grace.

Paul built bridges without compromising the message. He started where the people were, recognizing their search for meaning, and led them to the God who created everything, gives life, and now calls all people to repentance through His risen Son. His sermon at the Areopagus shows that the gospel can be clearly preached even in the most skeptical settings when we depend on the wisdom and courage of the Spirit.

Some mocked him, some hesitated, and others believed. That pattern still exists today. The mission of Christ isn't measured by how many accept but by how faithfully we speak. God equips us to engage our world with understanding, to reason with love, and to call others to truth. Like Paul, we must see our world not as a battlefield to be feared but as a mission field to be reached.

Memory Verse and Weekly Challenge

For as I was passing through and observing the objects of your worship, I even found an altar on which was inscribed: To an Unknown God. Therefore, what you worship in ignorance, this I proclaim to you.
Acts 17:23 (CSB)

Weekly Challenge: Find one moment to engage someone in meaningful conversation about faith. Listen first, then ask questions. Like Paul, gently steer the discussion toward understanding who God is and what He has done in Christ. Pray for courage to speak with clarity and love, trusting the Spirit to open hearts.

For Discussion

1. What do you think Paul felt as he looked at the idols throughout Athens? How does that compare to how you feel about today's culture?

   _____

   _____

   _____

2. How did Paul's approach at the Areopagus differ from how he preached in the synagogues, and what can we learn from that?

   _____

   _____

   _____

3. Why is it important to build bridges of understanding when sharing the gospel instead of immediately condemning others' beliefs?

   _____

   _____

   _____

4. What truths about God did Paul emphasize to correct the Athenians' false ideas?

   _____

   _____

   _____

5. How can you follow Paul's example in your workplace, neighborhood, or daily conversations—speaking truth with both conviction and compassion?

_____
_____
_____

Equipped a Young Church:
Paul in Corinth
Acts 18

Do not be afraid, but keep on speaking and don't be silent.
For I am with you, and no one will lay a hand on you to hurt you,
because I have many people in this city.
Acts 18:9–10

Class Overview: After leaving Athens, Paul traveled to Corinth, a city known for its wealth, trade, and corruption. It was a tough place to start a church, but God had great plans for it. In Corinth, Paul found new partners in ministry, faced strong opposition, and received encouraging words from the Lord. Through hard work, faithful teaching, and patient endurance, he helped build one of the most influential churches in the early days of the church. This lesson shows how God equips His servants to strengthen young believers, persevere through challenges, and rely on His presence amid discouragement.

Class Objectives: By the end of this class, you should be able to—

1. Describe the cultural and moral challenges of Corinth and how they affected Paul's ministry.
2. Explain how God provided encouragement and support to Paul through friends and fellow workers.
3. Understand how God's promise of presence gave Paul courage to keep preaching in a difficult environment.
4. Recognize the importance of mentoring and strengthening new believers.
5. Apply these lessons by trusting God to work through hardship and by investing in others' spiritual growth.

Introduction

WHEN PAUL ARRIVED IN CORINTH, he entered one of the most
challenging cities of the ancient world. It was a place full of opportunities
and temptations; a wealthy trade hub known for its immorality, pride,
and idol worship. The city sat at the crossroads of commerce, drawing
in merchants, travelers, and sailors from across the empire. It was also
home to the temple of Aphrodite, where hundreds of priestesses took
part in ritual prostitution as part of their religion. Corinth was a city
where pleasure was celebrated, and truth was often overlooked.

For a weary missionary fresh from the intellectual debates of Athens,
Corinth must have seemed overwhelming. Paul later described his
mindset when he first arrived: *I came to you in weakness, in fear, and in
much trembling.* (1 Corinthians 2:3). Yet, it was in this tough place that
God accomplished some of His greatest work.

In Corinth, Paul found support and companionship in Aquila and
Priscilla, Jewish tentmakers who had recently been expelled from Rome.
They shared his trade and faith, and their friendship became a source of
strength. Week after week, Paul preached in the synagogue, reasoning
with both Jews and Greeks that Jesus is the Christ. But as opposition
grew, discouragement set in; until one night the Lord spoke to Paul in a
vision: *'Do not be afraid, but keep on speaking, and don't be silent. For I am
with you.'*

Those words renewed Paul's courage. He stayed in Corinth for a year
and a half, teaching God's word and strengthening the believers. The
result was the formation of a strong, growing church in one of the most
unlikely places. This passage reminds us that God's mission continues
beyond dark or difficult environments. The same Spirit who sent Paul
to Corinth equips us today to serve faithfully, even when the culture is
tough, the work is slow, and the challenges are many.

Historical Background

Corinth was one of the most important and wealthy cities in the Roman
Empire. Rebuilt by Julius Caesar in 44 B.C. after being destroyed a
century earlier, it quickly became a busy commercial center. Located on

the narrow isthmus connecting mainland Greece to the Peloponnese, Corinth controlled two harbors: Lechaion on the west and Cenchreae on the east, which made it a vital point for trade, travel, and culture.

The city was cosmopolitan and wealthy but also deeply immoral. Ancient writers used the expression *"to Corinthianize"* to describe living in debauchery or sexual excess. The temple of Aphrodite sat high on the Acrocorinth, with priestesses participating in prostitution as part of pagan worship. Corinth was also filled with temples dedicated to other gods and was known for arrogance, greed, and vice.

Paul arrived there around A.D. 50 during his second missionary journey. After working in Macedonia and Athens, he arrived in Corinth exhausted physically and burdened emotionally. However, God had already prepared the way. He met Aquila and Priscilla, Jewish believers recently driven out of Rome by Emperor Claudius. They were tentmakers by trade and invited Paul to stay and work with them. Their partnership grew into a lifelong friendship and ministry team that later influenced churches in Ephesus and Rome.

Paul began his ministry in Corinth by teaching in the synagogue every Sabbath. As opposition increased, he moved to preaching to the Gentiles in the house of Titius Justus, a God-fearing man nearby. Among those who believed was Crispus, the synagogue leader, whose faith encouraged many others to believe and be baptized.

During this time, Paul likely felt fear and exhaustion, unsure how much longer he could go on. But one night, the Lord appeared to him in a vision: *"Do not be afraid, but keep on speaking and don't be silent. For I am with you, and no one will lay a hand on you to hurt you, because I have many people in this city."* (vv. 9–10). Empowered by that promise, Paul stayed in Corinth for eighteen months—the longest period of his second journey.

The gospel's influence extended beyond Corinth as well. Later in Acts 18, Luke introduces Apollos, a talented preacher from Alexandria who arrived in Ephesus. Although passionate and articulate, he only understood John's baptism. Aquila and Priscilla privately took him aside and taught him more accurately about Jesus. His humility and their patience demonstrated the kind of teamwork that bolsters young churches and prepares future leaders.

Corinth was a challenging place to preach, but it ultimately demonstrated God's grace in action. The church Paul founded there faced struggles with pride and division, yet it also served as a testament to God's power to bring light into dark places.

Equipped through God's Provision (18:1–6)

When Paul arrived in Corinth, he was tired, discouraged, and financially limited. Yet God had already arranged everything he needed. He met Aquila and Priscilla, Jewish tentmakers who had recently left Rome because of Emperor Claudius's decree expelling the Jews. They not only shared Paul's trade but also shared his faith. In their home and workshop, Paul found both friendship and stability. What started as a business partnership grew into a spiritual partnership that would last for years.

Paul worked with his hands during the week and debated in the synagogue every Sabbath, *trying to persuade both Jews and Greeks.* (v. 4). Even in hardship, he remained faithful to the mission. God's provision didn't eliminate Paul's effort; it supported him in it. The Lord provides not so we can take a break from service, but so we can serve longer and more effectively.

But opposition soon arose. When the Jews rejected his message and became abusive, Paul symbolically shook out his clothes in protest, saying, *"Your blood is on your own heads; I am innocent." From then on, I will go to the Gentiles.* (v. 6). This act was not out of bitterness; it was obedience. Paul understood his responsibility: to share the gospel faithfully and leave the results to God.

Immediately after this confrontation, Paul moved next door to the house of Titius Justus, a Gentile worshiper of God. His proximity to the synagogue showed that Paul had not given up on his people; he simply followed where God opened doors. One of the first converts after this shift was Crispus, the ruler of the synagogue, along with his entire household. Many others in Corinth believed and were baptized.

God's hand of provision is evident in every part of this story: through friendships, opportunities, and even rejection. The Spirit empowered

Paul to trust that when one door closed, another would open. The Lord's provision often comes through people placed in our path for encouragement and partnership. When we walk by faith, we begin to see that every relationship, every resource, and even every setback can be part of how God equips us to serve.

Equipped through God's Presence
(18:7–17)

After leaving the synagogue, Paul moved next door to Titius Justus's home, a Gentile Christian. From there, the gospel continued to spread. God's grace reached even into the synagogue as Crispus, the synagogue leader, and his household believed and were baptized. This victory was significant because it showed that the message of Christ could still soften hardened hearts. However, Paul's growing success also stirred up hostility. The tension from ongoing conflict likely exhausted him, and he may have wondered if it was time to move on.

Then God spoke. One night, the Lord appeared to Paul in a vision and said, *Do not be afraid, but keep on speaking and don't be silent. For I am with you, and no one will lay a hand on you to hurt you, because I have many people in this city.* (vv. 9–10). Those words renewed Paul's courage. He had faced rejection, persecution, and loneliness, but now God reminded him that he was not alone. The promise of divine presence, "I am with you," was the same assurance God gave Moses, Joshua, and the prophets. It's the same promise Jesus gave to His disciples: *I am with you always, to the end of the age.* (Matthew 28:20)

Encouraged by that assurance, Paul stayed in Corinth for a year and a half, teaching God's word. His longest stay up to that point became one of his most fruitful. Even when opposition resurfaced, God demonstrated His protection. The Jews brought Paul before Gallio, the Roman proconsul, accusing him of breaking the law. But Gallio dismissed the case, refusing to involve the Roman government in Jewish religious disputes. This legal precedent provided protection for Christian preaching across the empire for years afterward.

God's presence doesn't always eliminate problems. Instead, it gives us strength to endure them. Paul didn't avoid opposition, but he was prepared to face it with peace and confidence. When we remember that God is with us, fear loses its hold, and faith grows stronger. The Lord's presence isn't just a feeling; it's a fact. And it forms the foundation of all lasting ministry.

Equipped to Strengthen Others (18:18–28)

After a year and a half of ministry in Corinth, Paul set sail for Syria, accompanied by Priscilla and Aquila, his trusted coworkers. Their partnership was built through shared labor, faith, and perseverance. In Ephesus, Paul briefly preached in the synagogue before leaving for Caesarea and returning to Antioch, marking the end of his second missionary journey. However, his influence persisted through those he had trained and encouraged.

While Paul moved on, Priscilla and Aquila stayed in Ephesus. There, they met Apollos, a Jew from Alexandria who was eloquent, educated, and passionate about his teaching. He spoke confidently about the Scriptures and the coming Messiah but only knew the message of John the Baptist. Although sincere, his understanding was not complete.

Instead of publicly correcting him, Priscilla and Aquila invited Apollos into their home and *explained the way of God to him more accurately.* (v. 26). Their quiet wisdom and humility offer a timeless example of how mature believers support younger ones in truth. Apollos gratefully received their instruction and went on to become a powerful preacher, greatly aiding the believers in Achaia and defending the faith with conviction.

This final scene captures the essence of Christian leadership: disciples training disciples. Paul strengthened Aquila and Priscilla; they, in turn, trained Apollos, who then encouraged others. That is how the church grows—through faithful people passing on what they have learned.

In every season of ministry, God calls His servants not only to proclaim truth but also to reproduce it in others. The Spirit equips us to teach patiently, correct gently, and invest intentionally in the next generation of believers. Whether we lead a class, teach a child, or encourage a struggling friend, our goal remains the same: to strengthen others in faith so that the gospel continues to spread long after we have moved on.

Lesson Summary and Reflection

Key Truths from Corinth:

- God provides the right people, resources, and opportunities to sustain His servants in challenging work.
- The Lord's presence gives courage when opposition or fear sets in.
- Ministry grows stronger through partnerships built on faith and humility.
- Teaching and mentoring others are essential to equipping the church.
- God's mission continues through ordinary believers who faithfully invest in others.

Corinth was one of the toughest places Paul ever ministered, but it also became one of his greatest successes. What started with exhaustion and fear ended with a thriving church, loyal friends, and future leaders ready for service. Through every challenge, God provided Paul with what he needed most: His provision, His presence, and His people.

Paul's story in Corinth reminds us that God never sends His servants into the field unprepared. He provided work, friendship, and encouragement through Aquila and Priscilla. He strengthened Paul's courage with His promise, *"Do not be afraid, for I am with you."* And He produced lasting results: new believers, developing leaders, and a congregation that would later become a vital voice in the early church.

The Spirit also worked through Priscilla and Aquila, who patiently guided Apollos in the truth, illustrating that teaching and mentoring are vital parts of building strong churches. Ministry is never meant to be a solo effort. God surrounds His people with others to help share the burden and carry on the work.

We need consistent perseverance and collaboration. During times of discouragement or opposition, we can find comfort in knowing that God is always present, constantly working, and continually preparing others to stand with us. The Spirit empowers believers not just to endure ministry but to multiply it, ensuring the gospel continues to grow long after we're gone.

Memory Verse and Weekly Challenge

Do not be afraid, but keep on speaking and don't be silent.
For I am with you, and no one will lay a hand on you to hurt you,
because I have many people in this city.
Acts 18:9–10 (CSB)

Weekly Challenge: When you feel tired or discouraged in your work for the Lord, remember God's promise to Paul. Spend time this week praying for courage and endurance. Look for one person you can encourage or mentor in faith: someone who needs the reminder that God is with them too.

For Discussion

1. How did God provide for Paul's needs, physically, emotionally, and spiritually, while he served in Corinth?

    _____

    _____

    _____

2. What does Paul's vision in vv. 9–10 teach us about God's presence in times of fear or discouragement?

    _____

    _____

    _____

3. How do Aquila, Priscilla, and Apollos demonstrate the importance of mentoring and teamwork in ministry?

    _____

    _____

    _____

4. Why do you think God often chooses to work through relationships rather than through solitary effort?

    _____

    _____

    _____

5. What steps can you take this week to strengthen and encourage someone in their faith, as Paul did in Corinth?

_____

_____

_____

Equipped to Shepherd:
Paul to the Ephesian Elders
Acts 20:17–38

Be on guard for yourselves and for all the flock of which the Holy Spirit has appointed you as overseers, to shepherd the church of God, which he purchased with his own blood.
Acts 20:28

Class Overview: Acts 20 highlights one of the most personal and heartfelt moments in Paul's ministry. On his way to Jerusalem, he stopped at Miletus and called for the elders of the church in Ephesus to meet him there. Knowing this might be his final time with them, Paul delivered a moving farewell filled with instruction, warning, and encouragement. His message offers one of the clearest pictures in Scripture of what it means to shepherd God's people with integrity and courage. This lesson emphasizes how God equips leaders to care for His flock, guard against false teachings, and serve with humility, sacrifice, and love.

Class Objectives: By the end of this class, you should be able to—

1. Summarize the key themes of Paul's farewell message to the Ephesian elders.
2. Understand the biblical role and responsibility of church leaders as shepherds of God's flock.
3. Recognize the importance of humility, perseverance, and personal example in leadership.
4. Identify the dangers of false teaching and the need for spiritual vigilance.
5. Apply Paul's example by serving others with sincerity and faithfulness, trusting that the Lord's approval matters most.

Introduction

FEW PASSAGES IN ACTS REVEAL PAUL'S HEART like his farewell to the elders of Ephesus. For three years, he had lived among them, teaching, praying, and building a community in one of the most influential cities of the ancient world. The Ephesian church had become a model of faith and strength, but Paul knew challenges were ahead. As he traveled toward Jerusalem, where hardships awaited, he stopped at Miletus and asked the elders to meet him. What followed was not a formal speech but a shepherd's final plea to those who would carry on his work.

Paul's message was both heartfelt and practical. He reminded the elders of how he had served: with humility, tears, and perseverance through trials. He urged them to continue shepherding God's church, which was bought with Christ's blood, warning that false teachers would appear from both outside and inside the congregation. His love for them shone through in every word and in his final prayer as they wept together on the shore.

Here we see one of the clearest biblical depictions of spiritual leadership. A genuine shepherd doesn't lead for power or praise but for the benefit of the flock. He protects, nourishes, and guides God's people with compassion and conviction. Paul's example reminds us that ministry isn't about titles or authority—it's about service, character, and faithfulness to the truth. These days, when leadership often reflects worldly ambition, Acts 20 reminds us to focus on Christlike ministry. God equips shepherds not through comfort or prestige but through humility, endurance, and deep love for His people.

Historical Background

Ephesus was one of the most important cities in the Roman Empire: a thriving port on the western coast of Asia Minor (modern-day Turkey). Known for its commerce, culture, and the magnificent temple of Artemis (one of the Seven Wonders of the Ancient World), Ephesus was both influential and deeply pagan. Paul spent more time there than anywhere else during his missionary work—about three years (Acts 20:31). His ministry transformed the city. The gospel spread throughout the region, idol makers lost business, and the name of Jesus became known far beyond its borders.

By the time of Acts 20, Paul's third missionary journey was nearing its end. He was headed to Jerusalem to deliver a collection for the poor saints there, and he felt that imprisonment and suffering awaited him (Acts 20:22–23). Still, his concern for the Ephesian church led him to stop at Miletus, about thirty miles south of Ephesus, and call for the elders to meet him.

These elders, also known as overseers or shepherds, had been appointed to lead and care for the congregation Paul established. His farewell message to them is the only speech in Acts directly addressed to believers rather than unbelievers, offering a unique view of early church leadership priorities. Paul reminded them of his example: humble service, tireless teaching, and willingness to endure suffering for the sake of the gospel. He then urged them to continue that same work—guard the flock, protect it from false teachers, and rely entirely on God's grace.

Ephesus later faced the very challenges Paul predicted. False teachers emerged, causing division and spiritual decline. Decades afterward, Jesus Himself addressed the Ephesian church in Revelation 2:1–7, praising its endurance but warning that it had lost its first love. Paul's words in Acts 20 thus remain both relevant and timeless—a reminder that the health of any congregation depends on shepherds who serve faithfully, guard truth diligently, and love deeply.

Equipped by Example
(20:17–21)

Paul began his message to the Ephesian elders by pointing to his own example. *You know, from the first day I set foot in Asia, how I was with you the whole time, serving the Lord with all humility, with tears, and during the trials that came to me through the plots of the Jews.* (vv. 18–19). His ministry was not built on pride, authority, or appearance; it was marked by humility, compassion, and endurance.

He didn't just tell others how to live; he showed them. His actions were the greatest lesson he could leave behind. He served during difficult times, remained faithful despite persecution, and kept teaching even when it cost him dearly. Authentic leadership isn't about position or power; it's about consistency, integrity, and sincere love for God and His people.

Paul reminded them that he *did not hesitate to proclaim anything profitable to you or to teach you publicly and from house to house.* (v. 20). His ministry was open and personal. He preached at public gatherings and visited people in their homes, meeting them where they were. He held nothing back that would strengthen their faith.

His message was the same for everyone: *repentance toward God and faith in our Lord Jesus.* (v. 21). Whether Jew or Gentile, rich or poor, the gospel he preached focused on Christ and was rooted in grace. Paul's approach to ministry was simple yet powerful: truth conveyed with humility, love demonstrated through sacrifice, and perseverance shown through suffering.

For today's leaders, Paul's example sets the standard. Shepherds are called not only to teach sound doctrine but also to live it out. The church learns just as much from what its leaders do as from what they say. God equips His servants through experience, testing, and faithful endurance, so that their lives serve as visible testimonies of His grace. Paul's integrity gave more weight to his words. His life matched his message. That is what true leadership looks like: faithfulness over time, humility in service, and a heart that consistently cares for others' souls.

Equipped to Guard the Flock
(20:22–31)

After recalling his example, Paul turned to the serious charge that every shepherd must accept: to guard the flock. He told the elders that he was going to Jerusalem, driven *by the Spirit,* knowing that imprisonment and hardship awaited him (v. 22). Still, he declared, *I consider my life of no value to myself; my purpose is to finish my course and the ministry I received from the Lord Jesus, to testify to the gospel of God's grace.* (v. 24). That statement captures the heart of every faithful servant. Paul's priority was not safety or comfort but obedience. His life belonged to the One who called him. That same devotion is what equips leaders to stand firm when the work becomes difficult or dangerous.

Then Paul issued a serious warning: *Be on guard for yourselves and for all the flock, of which the Holy Spirit has made you overseers, to shepherd the church of God, which He bought with His own blood.* (v. 28). Leaders must first guard their own hearts before they can guard others. Spiritual vigilance begins with personal integrity—monitoring our attitudes, motives, and example.

The responsibility of shepherding is sacred. The church does not belong to any man; it belongs to God, bought with the blood of His Son. Because of that, leaders must be alert to threats from both outside and inside. Paul warned that *savage wolves will come in among you, not sparing the flock.* (v. 29). False teachers would arise, distorting truth to draw followers after themselves. The danger was not only doctrinal but also personal: selfish ambition masquerading as ministry.

Paul reminded them how he had served day and night with tears, warning and teaching everyone. His heart for the flock was caring and pastoral. He didn't just defend truth; he nurtured souls. A good shepherd observes, teaches patiently, and corrects with love.

Guarding the church is more than defending doctrine: it's about protecting people. The role of the shepherd is to keep the truth clear, love strong, and the flock safe from anything that could harm their faith. God equips leaders for this task through His Spirit, His Word, and the example of Christ, the Chief Shepherd who laid down His life for the sheep.

Equipped to Give and Bless
(20:32–38)

As Paul finished his farewell message, he entrusted the elders to the care and grace of God. *And now I commit you to God and to the word of his grace, which is able to build you up and give you an inheritance among all who are sanctified.* (v. 32). Paul knew he could not stay to protect them personally, but he trusted in the power of God's word to strengthen and sustain them. A shepherd's ultimate confidence is not in himself, but in the grace of God.

Paul reminded them of his example of generosity and self-sacrifice. *I have not coveted anyone's silver, gold, or clothing. You know that I worked with my own hands to support myself and those with me.* (vv. 33–34). He had not served for profit or recognition. His integrity contrasted with that of false teachers who used religion for personal gain. Instead, Paul labored hard, showing that true ministry gives more than it takes.

He summed up his life's principle in one powerful statement: *It is more blessed to give than to receive.* (v. 35). Although not recorded elsewhere in Scripture, these words reflect the heart of Jesus. Leadership in God's kingdom is about giving giving time, energy, compassion, truth, and prayer for others. A mature shepherd is characterized by a generous heart that mirrors the character of Christ.

After these final words, Paul knelt and prayed with everyone. The scene is tender and emotional: *They all wept loudly, and, throwing their arms around Paul, they kissed him, grieving most of all over his statement that they would never see his face again.* (v. 37–38). Their tears showed the love and respect they had for him. Paul's ministry had not just built a church; it had built relationships grounded in Christlike love.

Here we see the essence of servant leadership. Paul gave everything he had: his strength, his tears, his time, his heart. God had equipped him not just to lead but to love, not just to teach but to bless. The church still needs shepherds like that—leaders who rely on God's grace, serve without greed, and measure success not by what they gain but by how much they give.

Lesson Summary and Reflection

Key Truths from Ephesus:

- God equips leaders through humility, endurance, and faithfulness to His word.
- Shepherds must guard both their own hearts and the flock entrusted to them.
- The church belongs to God, purchased with the blood of His Son, and must be protected with care.

- Ministry that reflects Christ is marked by generosity, not greed, by service, not status.
- True leadership gives more than it receives and measures success by love and faithfulness.

Paul's farewell to the Ephesian elders stands as one of the most touching and instructive passages in the New Testament. It reveals the heart of a true shepherd; one who serves humbly, guards faithfully, and gives selflessly. His words remind us that leadership in the church is not about position or prestige, but about service and sacrifice.

Paul's life served as a lesson to others. He demonstrated endurance, a dedication to truth, and a deep compassion for God's people through his actions. He faced trials, tears, and persecution, yet he never stopped preaching the gospel of grace. His commitment to God's Word and his willingness to suffer for others set an example for all generations of church leaders.

He also urged the elders to protect the flock diligently, aware that false teachers would arise. The church needed leaders with courage and discernment—those who would defend sound doctrine and keep their hearts pure. But Paul didn't leave them to face this challenge alone. He committed them to God and the word of His grace, trusting that divine strength would sustain them when human effort falls short.

Finally, Paul reminded them that ministry is about giving, not gaining. The greatest joy in serving Christ comes from what we give, not what we receive. His farewell ended in tears, not from regret but from love. He had dedicated his life to the flock, and they had become his family. Every Christian, not just elders, must share the same spirit of faithfulness. God equips His people to serve with humility, perseverance, and love. Whether we lead a class, shepherd a family, or serve quietly, we are all called to mirror the heart of Christ, the Good Shepherd who laid down His life for His sheep.

Memory Verse and Weekly Challenge

Be on guard for yourselves and for all the flock of which the Holy Spirit has appointed you as overseers, to shepherd the church of God, which he purchased with his own blood.
Acts 20:28 (CSB)

Weekly Challenge: This week, pray for your church's shepherds and teachers. Offer them a note or word of encouragement. If you lead others, follow Paul's example and lead with greater humility.

For Discussion

1. What qualities in Paul's ministry stand out as examples for anyone serving in leadership or ministry today?

    _____

    _____

    _____

2. Why is humility such an essential part of spiritual leadership?

    _____

    _____

    _____

3. How can church leaders and members alike stay alert to the dangers Paul warned about in vv. 28–31?

    _____

    _____

    _____

4. What does Paul's statement, "It is more blessed to give than to receive," teach us about the heart of ministry?

    _____

    _____

    _____

5. How can you apply Paul's example this week in how you serve, encourage, or care for others?

    _____

    _____

    _____

Equipped to Defend the Faith: Paul's Trials

Acts 22–26

So then, King Agrippa, I was not disobedient to the heavenly vision
Acts 26:19

Class Overview: From his arrest in Jerusalem to his final hearing before King Agrippa, Paul faced rulers, soldiers, and councils—defending both his faith and his mission. Throughout every trial, he remained calm, courageous, and confident in the gospel. Instead of viewing his imprisonment as a setback, Paul saw it as a platform to share Christ with influential audiences. This lesson illustrates how God equips His servants to stand firm under pressure, give a reason for their hope, and turn opposition into opportunity. Paul's example shows believers that our faith is most convincing when it is lived and spoken with integrity, boldness, and grace.

Class Objectives:

By the end of this class, you should be able to:

1. Summarize Paul's primary defenses before the Jewish leaders, Felix, Festus, and King Agrippa.
2. Understand how Paul used his personal testimony as a tool for sharing the gospel.
3. Recognize how the Holy Spirit equips believers to speak with courage and clarity under pressure.
4. Identify lessons from Paul's example for responding to criticism, hostility, or injustice.
5. Apply these principles by learning to share personal faith stories that point others to Christ.

Introduction

FROM THE MOMENT PAUL RETURNED TO JERUSALEM, his journey was marked by conflict. False accusations, angry crowds, and unfair treatment followed him everywhere. Still, through it all, God's hand remained steady. What seemed like defeat turned into a series of divine opportunities. Paul wasn't just on trial for his life; he was standing as a witness for the gospel before rulers and kings.

When the Jews accused him of defiling the temple, Paul remained calm and defended himself. He shared his background as a Pharisee, his passion for the law, and his dramatic conversion on the road to Damascus. Every time he appeared before a new audience—whether the Sanhedrin, Governor Felix, Festus, or King Agrippa—Paul used the moment to tell his story and to honor Jesus as the risen Lord.

Paul's defenses show how a Christian can face pressure with courage. He didn't panic or fight back. He spoke honestly, respectfully, and confidently. Even when his audience mocked or rejected him, he stayed focused on his mission: to testify about what he had seen and heard. The same Spirit that strengthened him during his missionary trips now helped him stand firm in chains.

Acts 22–26 show that faith under pressure is one of the strongest testimonies of all. Paul's calm confidence in God displayed a peace that no court could take away. His life reminds us that defending the faith isn't just about answering arguments—it's about demonstrating the power of the gospel through steadfast trust and clear witness. When we live faithfully under pressure, we become living proof that Christ is real and that His grace is enough in every trial. *God himself will be with them and will be their God.* That is the promise. Heaven will be heaven because we will live in the eternal presence of God.

Historical Background

Paul's trials happen during the final years of his third missionary journey and at the start of his long trip to Rome. Around A.D. 57, he returned to Jerusalem after years of ministry among the Gentiles, bringing a collection from the churches to support the poor saints there. His arrival caused controversy. Jewish leaders accused him of teaching against the law of Moses and of defiling the temple by bringing Gentiles into its courts—charges that were both false and inflammatory.

A riot erupted in the temple area, and Roman soldiers stepped in to prevent the mob from beating Paul to death. The commander, Claudius Lysias, arrested Paul and allowed him to address the crowd. From the steps of the fortress (Acts 22), Paul gave his testimony in Hebrew, describing his past as a persecutor of Christians and his encounter with Jesus on the road to Damascus. His mention of being sent to the Gentiles sparked the crowd's fury again, prompting the Romans to take him inside for his safety.

The next day, Paul stood before the Jewish Sanhedrin (Acts 23). Recognizing that his audience was split between Pharisees and Sadducees, he strategically emphasized his belief in the resurrection. This led to disagreement, and the Roman commander removed him again for his safety. That night, the Lord appeared to Paul and said, *Have courage! For as you have testified about me in Jerusalem, so it is necessary for you to testify in Rome.* (Acts 23:11)

From Jerusalem, Paul was moved to Caesarea for trial before Governor Felix (Acts 24). Felix was interested in Paul's message but postponed judgment, hoping for a bribe. Two years later, when Festus took over from Felix, Paul again defended himself against Jewish accusations (Acts 25). When Festus suggested sending him back to Jerusalem for trial, Paul used his right as a Roman citizen and appealed to Caesar.

Before being sent to Rome, Paul made a final defense before King Agrippa II and his sister Bernice (Acts 26). In this powerful scene, Paul again shared his testimony and boldly declared Christ's resurrection. Agrippa famously replied, *"Are you going to persuade me to become a Christian so easily?"* (26:28). Although the rulers found him innocent, Paul's appeal to Caesar meant he would be sent to Rome, just as the Lord had promised.

God used imprisonment and injustice to bring Paul before rulers, governors, and kings. Each hearing became a platform for the gospel. What seemed like the end of Paul's freedom was actually the start of the gospel's spread into the heart of the empire.

Equipped with a Clear Testimony
(22:1–21)

Standing on the steps of the fortress in Jerusalem, surrounded by soldiers and an angry crowd, Paul asked for permission to speak. The situation was tense, yet he did not shout or retaliate. Instead, he calmly addressed the crowd as *brothers and fathers,* showing respect to those who despised him. When he began speaking in Hebrew, the crowd fell silent.

Paul's defense was clear and strong: he told his story. He reminded them that he was a Jew, born in Tarsus, educated under Gamaliel, and zealous for the law; just like they were. He explained how he once persecuted followers of Jesus, arresting and imprisoning them. But then came the turning point: the day he met the risen Christ on the road to Damascus.

He recounted how a bright light from heaven surrounded him and how he heard a voice saying, *Saul, Saul, why are you persecuting me?* When Paul asked who was speaking, the answer came: *I am Jesus of Nazareth, the one you are persecuting.* That single encounter changed everything. The persecutor became the preacher; the enemy became the servant.

Paul's testimony revealed both God's mercy and his mission. He described how Ananias came to him, restored his sight, and said, *'The God of our ancestors has chosen you to know his will, to see the Righteous One, and to hear the words from his mouth, since you will be a witness for him to all people.'* (vv. 14–15)

Then came the commission that defined the rest of his life: God sent him not only to his own people but also to the Gentiles. That statement again angered the crowd, but Paul's purpose was clear. He wanted them to understand that his faith was not rebellion; it was obedience to the God of Israel. Paul's example shows the power of a personal testimony. When explaining the gospel, he didn't rely solely on argument; he shared what Christ had done for him. Every believer can do the same. We may not all stand before crowds, but we all have a story of grace, a story that can open hearts to the truth. The Spirit equips us to speak it clearly, humbly, and boldly whenever the opportunity comes.

Equipped for Courage Under Pressure
(Acts 23–25)

Paul's defense before the Sanhedrin and the Roman governors shows remarkable courage under continuous pressure. He faced angry mobs, false accusations, and powerful men who could end his life with a single word, yet he never wavered. His strength came not from his own resolve but from his trust in God's plan.

When Paul stood before the Sanhedrin, he began by saying, *Brothers, I have lived my life before God in good conscience up to this day.* (23:1). His statement provoked anger, and the high priest ordered him to be struck on the mouth. Even then, Paul kept his composure, showing that conviction does not require hostility. When he saw that his audience was divided between Pharisees and Sadducees, he wisely highlighted the resurrection, the doctrine at the center of both his faith and their division. The uproar that followed forced the Roman commander to intervene once again.

That night, as Paul sat confined in the barracks, the Lord Himself appeared to him with reassurance: *'Have courage! For as you have testified about me in Jerusalem, so it is necessary for you to testify in Rome.'* (23:11). That promise became the anchor of Paul's heart. No matter what plots or trials came next, he knew God's purpose would not fail.

Over the next two years, Paul faced multiple hearings before Governor Felix, Festus, and the Jewish accusers who sought his execution. Felix delayed judgment, hoping for a bribe, while Festus tried to please the Jews by sending Paul back to Jerusalem for trial. Knowing the danger he faced there, Paul used his rights as a Roman citizen and appealed to Caesar. His decision ensured he would eventually take the gospel to Rome, fulfilling the Lord's promise.

Throughout all of this, Paul's courage relied on God's sovereignty. He didn't see himself as a victim but as an ambassador in chains. Every court became a platform, every hearing a pulpit. Even when people in power were corrupt or indifferent, Paul's faith never wavered. Courage in the Christian life does not mean the absence of fear. It means trusting God in the face of it. Paul's calm endurance reminds us that no circumstance, no authority, and no injustice can silence the message of Christ when the Spirit equips us to stand firm.

Equipped to Proclaim the Truth Boldly (26:1–32)

When Paul stood before King Agrippa, he faced one of the most dramatic moments of his life. He was in chains, surrounded by soldiers, rulers, and Roman officials, men of rank and influence. Yet Paul's tone was not fearful or defensive. He spoke with calm conviction, showing respect for the king while seizing the opportunity to proclaim the gospel.

I consider myself fortunate, Paul began, *that today I am going to make a defense before you… because you are very knowledgeable about all the Jewish customs and controversies.* (26:2–3). His words were gracious but confident. Instead of focusing on his suffering, he focused on his mission—to testify about Christ.

Once again, Paul recounted his story. He described his former life as a persecutor, his encounter with Jesus on the Damascus road, and the commission he received to preach to both Jews and Gentiles. In this retelling, Paul highlighted the message Christ had given him: *I am sending you to open their eyes so that they may turn from darkness to light and from the power of Satan to God, that they may receive forgiveness of sins and a share among those who are sanctified by faith in me.* (v. 18).

Then Paul declared the key statement that defined his entire ministry: *"So then, King Agrippa, I was not disobedient to the heavenly vision."* (v. 19). He had obeyed Christ's call, preaching repentance and faith wherever he went. Because of that, and not for any crime, he now faced trial.

Festus interrupted, accusing Paul of being insane because of his great learning. But Paul replied calmly, *I'm not out of my mind, most excellent Festus. On the contrary, I'm speaking words of truth and good judgment* (v. 25). Turning to Agrippa, Paul pressed the question home: *Do you believe the prophets? I know you believe* (v. 27). The king's reply was famous: *Are you going to persuade me to become a Christian so easily?* (v. 28).

Paul's answer reflects the heart of an evangelist: *I wish before God that, whether easily or with difficulty, not only you but all who listen to me today might become like me—except for these chains.* (v. 29). Even in captivity, Paul's desire was not for freedom but for others' salvation. When the hearing ended, the rulers agreed: Paul had done nothing deserving death or imprisonment. Yet because he had appealed to Caesar, he would continue his journey to Rome. Paul's defense before Agrippa demonstrates the courage and clarity that come from walking closely with God. He didn't see himself as a prisoner of Rome but as a servant of Christ, commissioned to speak truth wherever he was. The Spirit who strengthened Paul in that courtroom still equips believers today—to share our faith boldly, even when the world resists or ridicules it.

Lesson Summary and Reflection

Key Truths from Paul's Trials:

- God equips His people to speak with courage and clarity, even under pressure.
- A clear personal testimony is one of the strongest tools for sharing the gospel.
- The Spirit uses opposition and hardship to open doors for greater witness.
- True defense of the faith is shown not only in words but in steadfast character and grace.
- Every trial can become an opportunity for God's glory when we remain faithful to our calling.

Paul's trials before the Jewish leaders and Roman officials reveal a faith that could not be shaken. Though accused, beaten, and imprisoned, he never lost sight of his mission. His calm, respectful, and unwavering testimony turned every courtroom into a platform for the gospel. What others saw as defeat, Paul saw as divine opportunity.

Before angry mobs, skeptical governors, and curious kings, Paul stood as a man at peace because he knew whom he served. His testimony remained consistent in every setting—he once opposed Christ, but now he lived to proclaim Him. His strength came from the confidence that God's plan was still unfolding, even through chains.

Paul's example shows us that defending the faith is about more than just knowledge; it's about character. The Spirit empowers us to speak the truth with kindness, respond to hostility with patience, and view every challenge as an opportunity to lead others to Jesus. Our strongest witness often comes not in comfortable moments but in times of testing.

Like Paul, we are called to give an account of our hope, not with arrogance but with sincerity and love. Whether talking to a neighbor or facing opposition, our task remains the same: to demonstrate that the gospel is true because it has transformed us. When we live and speak with that kind of integrity, God uses our lives as living defenses of His truth.

Memory Verse and Weekly Challenge

So then, King Agrippa, I was not disobedient to the heavenly vision.
Acts 26:19 (CSB)

Weekly Challenge: Reflect on how God has influenced your life. Write down your personal testimony—how you came to faith, what Christ has changed in you, and the hope you now hold in Him. Pray for the courage to share part of that story with someone this week. Like Paul, let your life and words testify to the truth of the gospel.

For Discussion

1. How does Paul's example show that a clear personal testimony can be one of the most effective ways to share the gospel?

   _____

   _____

   _____

2. What stands out to you about Paul's courage and calmness during his trials before rulers and kings?

   _____

   _____

   _____

3. How did God use Paul's imprisonment and suffering to advance the message of Christ?

   _____

   _____

   _____

4. What lessons can we learn from Paul about responding to criticism, false accusation, or hostility with grace?

   _____

   _____

   _____

5. How can you prepare yourself to "give a defense" of your faith when opportunities arise in your own life?

   _____

   _____

   _____

Equipped for the Journey:
Paul's Voyage to Rome
Acts 27

But now I urge you to take courage,
because there will be no loss of any of your lives, but only of the ship.
Acts 27:22

Class Overview: Acts 27 narrates the intense journey of Paul heading to Rome—a trip filled with danger, delays, and setbacks. As a prisoner facing trial before Caesar, Paul was put on a ship with soldiers, sailors, and other prisoners. Soon, fierce winds and violent storms threatened everyone aboard. Yet, through it all, Paul stayed calm, confident, and brave because he trusted in God's promise that he would reach Rome. This chapter isn't just an adventure story; it offers a powerful lesson in faith, leadership, and God's care. It demonstrates how the Spirit empowers believers to stay strong, provide hope, and lead others through life's storms.

Class Objectives: By the end of this class, you should be able to—

1. Describe the main events and challenges of Paul's voyage to Rome in Acts 27.
2. Understand how Paul's faith and leadership provided stability in a time of crisis.
3. Recognize God's sovereign hand in protecting and fulfilling His purposes even through difficulty.
4. Identify the spiritual lessons about trust, endurance, and influence during life's storms.
5. Apply Paul's example by learning to stay anchored in faith and offer courage to others during trials.

Introduction

THE VOYAGE TO ROME IS ONE OF THE MOST VIVID AND DETAILED STORIES in the book of Acts. It reads like an eyewitness account, and it is. Luke was with Paul on this journey, recording every moment of the storm, the shipwreck, and the faith that carried them through it all.

Paul had appealed to Caesar, fulfilling the Lord's promise that he would testify in Rome. But the trip did not go as anyone had planned. What should have been a routine voyage became a desperate struggle against wind, waves, and fear. From the very beginning, delays and poor decisions set the stage for disaster. As the ship sailed late in the season, a violent storm known as the *northeaster* struck, driving them helplessly for days across the Mediterranean.

Amid the chaos, Paul remained the calmest person on board. Even though he was a prisoner in chains, he became the ship's true leader—encouraging, warning, and comforting those around him. When others lost hope, Paul offered words of courage: *Keep up your courage, because I believe God that it will be just the way it was told to me.* (v. 25). His faith in God's promise brought peace to everyone else on the ship.

Acts 27 is not just a record of ancient travel. Spiritually, it is a picture of how faith behaves in the storms of life. The same God who guided Paul through that storm still rules over ours. We all face seasons when the winds rise, the course is unclear, and we feel powerless to change our circumstances. Here we are reminded that God's purpose is never defeated by disaster. He equips His people to trust Him, speak hope, and lead others safely through the storm.

Historical Context

By the time of Acts 27, Paul had already spent several years in prison in Caesarea. After multiple hearings before Felix and Festus, and his appeal to Caesar, he was finally taken into Roman custody for transport to Rome. Traveling with him were Luke (the author of Acts) and Aristarchus, a fellow worker from Thessalonica (v. 2).

The voyage started in Caesarea, with the prisoners under the guard of Julius, a centurion of the Augustan Cohort, an officer known for his experience and integrity. Their journey would cover nearly 2,000 miles, stopping at Sidon, Myra, Cnidus, Fair Havens, and finally Malta after the shipwreck.

They set sail late in the season, probably in September or October, when sailing conditions on the Mediterranean became risky due to unpredictable winds and storms. Paul, a seasoned traveler who had already experienced shipwrecks before (see 2 Corinthians 11:25), warned that continuing the voyage could lead to great loss. Still, the pilot and shipowner, motivated by profit and optimism, decided to press on toward Phoenix, a better harbor for wintering.

Soon after, a fierce storm called the *Euroclydon* (a nor'easter) struck. The wind pushed the ship uncontrollably southwest toward the open sea. The sailors fought desperately, securing the ship with ropes, lowering anchors, and throwing cargo overboard, but after many days without sunlight or stars, they lost all hope of surviving.

In that darkest moment, Paul stood before them and spoke with confidence rooted in faith. An angel of God appeared to him, assuring him that even though the ship would be lost, everyone on board would be saved. Paul's words boosted the 276 people on the ship. They eventually ran aground on the island of Malta, just as God had promised.

Acts 27 is notable in ancient literature for its detailed account of seamanship, storms, and survival. But beyond the historical accuracy lies a deeper message: divine providence. Through danger and disaster, God remains in control. Paul's voyage reminds every believer that life's storms do not break God's promises—they are reaffirmed through them.

Equipped to Trust God's Direction (27:1–12)

When Paul set sail for Rome, he was not in control of the journey. As a prisoner under Roman authority, his life was in the hands of others. Yet even in chains, he stayed focused on God's guidance. From the very beginning, delays and obstacles appeared. The winds worked against them, and progress was slow. After changing ships at Myra, the voyage became even more difficult as they struggled to make their way along the southern coast of Crete.

When they reached a place called Fair Havens, Paul sensed impending danger. The season for safe sailing was nearly over. Using his experience and judgment, he warned the centurion and the ship's officers: *Men, I can see that this voyage is headed toward disaster and heavy loss, not only of the cargo and the ship but also of our lives.* (v. 10). However, his warning went unheeded. The pilot and shipowner persuaded the centurion to continue toward Phoenix, a better harbor for wintering.

Here we learn an important spiritual lesson: trusting God's guidance often involves speaking truth, even when others ignore it. Paul's insight was not based only on logic or weather patterns; it was rooted in spiritual sensitivity and wisdom gained from experience. The world judges success by skill, but God judges it by faithfulness.

Paul couldn't control the ship's course, but he stayed steady because he trusted the One who rules the sea. Even when others dismissed his advice, Paul's peace came from knowing that God was guiding his steps. Leadership isn't about controlling outcomes; it's about listening to God and doing what's right, regardless of who listens.

Sometimes God allows others to make choices that lead us into storms. Yet His sovereignty is never lost. Even when the ship sails into danger, He is still guiding the story. The Spirit equips us to trust that divine guidance is greater than human decision, and that God can use even wrong turns to fulfill His perfect plan.

Equipped to Endure the Storm (27:13–26)

Initially, it seemed that Paul's warning might have been unnecessary. A gentle south wind began to blow, and the sailors thought they had achieved their goal. Confident in their own judgment, they set sail close to the coast of Crete. But the calm did not last. Suddenly, a violent *nor'easter* swept down from the island. The ship was caught in the gale and couldn't face the wind, so they let it be driven along.

Very quickly, control was lost. The sailors worked desperately to secure the ship, passing ropes underneath it to hold it together, lowering the gear, and throwing cargo overboard. Day after day, the storm raged. The sky disappeared. Luke records that *for many days neither the sun nor the stars appeared, and the severe storm continued to rage. Finally, all hope of being saved was fading.* (v. 20) In that moment of despair, God's servant stood up. Paul had heard from heaven again. An angel of the Lord appeared to him and said, *"Don't be afraid, Paul. It is necessary for you to stand before Caesar." And indeed, God has graciously given you all those who are sailing with you.* (v. 24)

Armed with that promise, Paul brought calm to chaos. He spoke faith into fear: *So take courage, men, because I believe God that it will be just the way it was told to me.* (v. 25). Those words reveal the secret of endurance—believing God when circumstances seem impossible. The storm didn't stop right away. The waves kept crashing, and the ship still drifted, but Paul's heart was steady. Faith doesn't always stop the storm; it changes how we face it. The same God who saved Paul from mobs, trials, and prisons would now carry him through the sea.

Storms often become classrooms of faith. God equips His people not by keeping them from the storm, but by sustaining them through it. He uses the winds and waves to strip away false security so that we might learn to depend wholly on His word. When life feels out of control, faith rests in this truth: what God has promised, He will perform.

Equipped to Lead and Encourage Others (27:27–44)

After two grueling weeks at sea, the storm still raged on. The sailors had done everything they could, but now survival felt impossible. Yet in that darkness, Paul became the ship's calm voice. The prisoner had become the captain, not through authority, but through faith. His trust in God gave him influence with everyone on board.

As dawn approached, Paul urged everyone to eat, reminding them that God had promised their lives would be spared. *So, take courage, because none of you will lose a hair from your head.* (v. 34). Then, in a powerful moment of peace amid chaos, he took bread, gave thanks to God in front of them all, broke it, and began to eat (v. 35). This public act of worship was a visible reminder that faith still endures when everything else falls apart.

That simple act changed the atmosphere. *Everyone was encouraged and began to get food themselves,* (v. 36). Faith is contagious. One person's courage can inspire many others. God had placed Paul on that ship not only to survive the storm but to guide souls through it. Eventually, the sailors realized they were nearing land and released the anchors. The vessel ran aground on a sandbar, and the force of the waves shattered it. The soldiers planned to kill the prisoners to prevent their escape, but the centurion, Julius, stopped them, determined to save Paul's life. In the end, everyone reached land safely, just as God had promised.

Faith under pressure transforms into leadership during a crisis. Paul never sought control, but he led by example: through prayer, calmness, and trust. When others panicked, he believed; when they starved, he gave thanks; when they feared for their lives, he reminded them of God's promise. This illustrates what it means to be equipped by the Spirit: to stay steady when the world trembles, to point others to hope when none seems visible, and to trust that God's word will hold firm when everything else collapses. The same Lord who safely brought Paul ashore still guides His people through today's storms.

Lesson Summary and Reflection

Key Truths from Paul's Journey:

- Storms, delays, or human mistakes never hinder God's purposes.
- Faith is anchored in God's promises, not in favorable circumstances.
- The Spirit equips us to remain calm, courageous, and thankful during trials.
- One person's trust in God can bring courage and stability to many others.
- Every storm becomes a platform for God to display His faithfulness and power.

Acts 27 serves as an important reminder that faith doesn't prevent us from facing storms, but it does carry us through them. Paul's journey to Rome started as a prisoner's trip but became a testament to God's power, providence, and promises. Even though he had no control over the ship or the sea, Paul trusted the One who held authority over both.

When others lost hope, Paul remained steadfast because he had heard from God. His confidence was not in the crew, the centurion, or the ship's strength, but in the word of the Lord: *It will be just the way it was told to me.* That simple statement captures the essence of faith. Believing God's promises brings peace even when circumstances give no reason for hope.

Through Paul's calm leadership, the entire crew witnessed how faith can make a difference in a crisis. His prayers, encouragement, and gratitude transformed fear into courage. The storm that seemed ready to destroy them became the stage where God's faithfulness was revealed.

Every Christian will face seasons when the winds rise and life becomes unmanageable. God's presence remains constant even when our footing isn't. The Spirit equips us to endure hardship, speak hope when others despair, and lead others toward safety, not always to calm seas but to true salvation. The storm did not end Paul's mission; it carried him exactly where God planned. So it is with us. Every trial is part of the journey that shapes our faith, builds our trust, and points others to the unshakable anchor: Jesus Christ.

Memory Verse and Weekly Challenge

But now I urge you to take courage,
because there will be no loss of any of your lives, but only of the ship.
Acts 27:22 (CSB)

Weekly Challenge: When storms enter your life—whether emotional, spiritual, or physical—pause and remember God's promise to be with you. Read Acts 27:21–26 and thank Him for His constant presence. Then find someone who is struggling and encourage them. Share a word of faith or pray with them, reminding them that God's promises still stand true.

For Discussion

1. What does Paul's calm leadership during the storm teach us about faith under pressure?

   _____

   _____

   _____

2. Why do you think Paul's warnings were ignored at first? What lessons can we learn from that?

   _____

   _____

   _____

3. How did Paul's faith and words of encouragement impact the people on board the ship?

   _____

   _____

   _____

4. What promises from God have helped anchor you during life's storms?

   _____

   _____

   _____

5. How can you bring hope and stability to others when they are facing fear, confusion, or uncertainty?

   _____

   _____

   _____

Equipped for Ministry:
Paul on Malta and in Rome
Acts 28

He proclaimed the kingdom of God and taught about the Lord Jesus Christ
with all boldness and without hindrance
Acts 28:31.

Class Overview: After surviving the storm and shipwreck, Paul's journey to Rome continued under God's faithful care. Acts 28 recounts the final scenes of the book: the apostle's ministry on the island of Malta, his arrival in Rome, and his ongoing witness while under house arrest. Although still a prisoner, Paul was anything but silent. His words, actions, and endurance show that no circumstance can stop the work of the gospel. This lesson teaches that God equips His servants to serve effectively wherever they are—whether in hardship, limitation, or freedom—so that His kingdom advances "without hindrance."

Class Objectives: By the end of this class, you should be able to—

1. Describe Paul's ministry on Malta and how God used miracles to open hearts.
2. Explain how Paul's arrival and ministry in Rome fulfilled God's promise.
3. Recognize that gospel work continues regardless of personal limitation or circumstance.
4. Understand the importance of perseverance and faithfulness in ministry until life's end.
5. Apply Paul's example by remaining faithful and fruitful in whatever season or situation God places us..

Introduction

AFTER TWO WEEKS IN THE STORM AND A SHIPWRECK that nearly cost him his life, Paul and everyone aboard the vessel washed ashore safely in Malta, just as God had promised. Although cold, wet, and exhausted, they quickly received kindness from the islanders, who built a fire and welcomed them. What began as a tragedy turned into another opportunity for ministry.

As Paul gathered sticks for the fire, a viper bit his hand. The locals thought he must be a criminal whom justice had finally caught. But when Paul shook the snake into the fire and was unharmed, their fear turned to amazement. Soon, Paul was invited into the home of Publius, the island's chief official. When Publius' father was sick with a fever and dysentery, Paul prayed and healed him. Others on the island came, and God used Paul to bring healing and hope to many.

After three months in Malta, Paul and his companions finally set out for Rome. There, under house arrest, Paul received visitors, preached the gospel, and taught about God's kingdom for two full years. Although chained to a Roman guard, he remained spiritually free. His courage and conviction turned his confinement into a mission field.

The final chapter of Acts ends not with defeat but with victory. The gospel that began in Jerusalem has now reached the heart of the empire. Luke's closing words, spoken *boldly and without hindrance,* remind us that God's word cannot be chained. Paul's example encourages every Christian to keep serving faithfully, even when life doesn't go as planned. Ministry doesn't stop when circumstances change; it simply takes a new form.

Historical Background

After the shipwreck described in Acts 27, Paul and his companions, 276 people in total, found refuge on the island of Malta, located south of Sicily in the Mediterranean Sea. The name "Malta" probably comes from a Phoenician word meaning "refuge," which fits well with what God provided there. The people of the island, though pagan, were unusually kind. Luke calls them *unusual in kindness,* showing God's providence in surrounding Paul with compassion after months of danger.

Paul's miraculous survival from the viper bite quickly drew everyone's attention. The Maltese people believed in divine justice (possibly under the name "Dike"), so when Paul was unharmed, they concluded he was under divine favor. This opened the door for ministry, and soon Paul was invited to the home of Publius, the leading Roman official on the island. When Publius's father was ill, Paul prayed, laid hands on him, and healed him. The result was a flood of requests from the sick all over the island, and Paul ministered to many before leaving three months later.

In the spring, when sailing was safe again, they boarded an Alexandrian ship. Their journey took them north to Syracuse, Rhegium, and finally Puteoli, near Naples. From there, they traveled by land along the Appian Way toward Rome, greeted by groups of believers who came out to meet Paul at the Forum of Appius and Three Taverns. Their warm reception greatly encouraged him: *When Paul saw them, he thanked God and took courage.* (v. 15).

In Rome, Paul was placed under house arrest, guarded by a soldier but allowed to receive visitors freely. His first act was to meet with the Jewish leaders, explaining that he was imprisoned for the hope of Israel and that he had done nothing against the law or his people. Some believed, while others rejected the message. Yet Paul kept teaching anyone who would listen, Jews and Gentiles alike, about the kingdom of God and the Lord Jesus Christ.

Acts ends with Paul still under guard but fully active in his ministry. Luke's final words, *with all boldness and without hindrance,* serve as a fitting conclusion to the book. The gospel has triumphed. The kingdom of God has reached the world's capital, and no human authority can silence its message. The story of Acts concludes, but the mission of Christ continues. Every believer is called to the same boldness, perseverance, and faith that carried Paul from storm to shore to Rome.

Equipped to Serve Wherever God Leads (28:1–10)

When Paul and his companions washed up on Malta, they had nothing, no ship, no supplies, and no plan. Yet God had already prepared a new mission field. What seemed like a detour was actually divine guidance. Sometimes the Lord's greatest work happens in places we never planned to go.

The islanders showed remarkable kindness by building a fire to warm the soaked survivors. As Paul gathered sticks, a viper bit him. The locals assumed this was a sign of judgment, that Paul must be a murderer escaping the sea only to be struck by fate. But when he suffered no harm, their opinion changed instantly. They went from seeing him as cursed to viewing him as divine. Paul's calm response showed both faith and perspective. He didn't panic, boast, or explain. He simply trusted God and kept on serving.

Soon, Paul was invited into the home of Publius, the island's chief official. When Publius's father fell ill with fever and dysentery, Paul visited, prayed, laid his hands on him, and healed him. After this, others came from across the island to be healed as well. Through Paul's presence, the people of Malta saw the compassion and power of God. For three months, Paul ministered there, teaching, praying, healing, and serving. When it was time to leave, the islanders honored him and supplied everything needed for the rest of the journey. What began as a shipwreck became a season of fruitful ministry.

Ministry isn't restricted by location or circumstances. Whether shipwrecked or sheltered, in hardship or comfort, God can use His people anywhere. The Spirit equips us to serve faithfully in unexpected places, to see opportunity in inconvenience, and to demonstrate Christ's love through both words and actions. Every detour can be divine when we invite God to lead.

Equipped to Encourage and Build Up Others (28:11–16)

After three months on the island of Malta, the winter storms subsided and sailing became safe again. Paul and his companions boarded another ship from Alexandria and continued toward Italy. The vessel had a figurehead of the Twin Brothers, Castor and Pollux, sons of Zeus, believed to be protectors of sailors. Ironically, the true protection of that voyage came not from pagan gods but from the living God who had guided Paul every step of the way.

The ship briefly stopped at Syracuse in Sicily, then at Rhegium, and finally reached Puteoli, a major port near modern Naples. There, Paul found fellow Christians, a reminder that the gospel had already reached Italy before he arrived. Luke notes that these brothers and sisters welcomed them and invited them to stay for seven days. What must that have meant for Paul after months of hardship and travel? Christian fellowship refreshed his spirit and renewed his courage.

From Puteoli, Paul and his group started the final part of their journey along the Appian Way, the famous Roman road that leads to the capital. As they traveled, more believers came out to meet them at the Forum of Appius and Three Taverns, two well-known rest stops along the route. When Paul saw them, Luke records, *he thanked God and took courage.* (v. 15)

Even the strongest servants of God need encouragement. Paul, the great apostle and missionary, was still human. The sight of faithful believers waiting for him lifted his spirit. Ministry is never a solo journey. God strengthens His people through the presence, prayers, and fellowship of others.

When Paul finally reached Rome, he was allowed to live alone under guard. The chains were still there, but his mission went on. The Spirit had equipped him not only to endure the storm but to come out stronger through the love of fellow believers. God still works this way today, using encouragement and shared faith to renew our courage when the road feels long.

Equipped to Proclaim Without Hindrance (28:17–31)

When Paul reached Rome, he wasted no time continuing his mission. Though under house arrest and chained to a Roman guard, he remained free in spirit. Within three days, he called together the local Jewish leaders to explain his situation. He assured them that he had done nothing against his people or their customs, but that he was in chains because of *"the hope of Israel,"* (v. 20) the promise of the Messiah fulfilled in Jesus.

Some of the leaders were curious, so they arranged another meeting to learn more. On that day, *many came to him at his lodging.* From morning until evening, Paul explained the kingdom of God and tried to persuade them about Jesus using the Law of Moses and the Prophets (v. 23). Some were convinced, while others refused to believe. Paul reminded them of Isaiah's prophecy, that hearts would grow dull and ears be deaf to the truth, but he also declared that God's salvation had now been sent to the Gentiles, and they would listen.

Not even rejection could stop the gospel. Luke concludes the book of Acts with these words: *Paul stayed two whole years in his own rented house. And he welcomed all who visited him, proclaiming the kingdom of God and teaching about the Lord Jesus Christ with all boldness and without hindrance.* (vv. 30–31). That phrase, *without hindrance,* is striking. Paul was confined, yet the gospel was not. The Roman guards who rotated shifts in his house heard the message of Christ. Visitors came and left encouraged. Letters written during this time—like Ephesians, Philippians, Colossians, and Philemon—would go on to strengthen generations of believers.

Acts does not end with closure but with continuation. The story of the church does not stop at Paul's imprisonment; it continues through every believer who carries the message forward. Walls, chains, or governments have never limited God's mission. Wherever His people live, in freedom or under restriction, He equips them to proclaim His word boldly and faithfully. Paul's example calls us to the same commitment. Ministry doesn't depend on perfect circumstances. We can serve, teach, and influence others wherever God places us. The gospel is still advancing today, "without hindrance," through all who trust and obey the Lord's call.

Lesson Summary and Reflection

Key Truths from Malta and Rome:

- God turns detours and delays into new opportunities for ministry.
- The Spirit equips believers to serve faithfully, even in hardship or limitation.
- Encouragement and fellowship strengthen courage for the work ahead.
- The gospel cannot be chained—God's word advances "without hindrance."
- Faithful service in every season leaves a lasting impact on the kingdom of God.

Acts 28 concludes Paul's journey and the book of Acts with a victorious note. What began with a storm ended with the gospel firmly planted in the heart of the Roman Empire. Throughout every trial, God's faithfulness shines through. Paul never reached Rome in comfort, but he arrived in victory, bringing the message of Christ to places no one could have foreseen.

In Malta, God used Paul's compassion and faith to open hearts through healing and service. In Rome, God granted him influence even while he was chained. Every obstacle became an opportunity for ministry. Paul's faithfulness demonstrates that the effectiveness of ministry is never based on our freedom or environment but on our willingness to serve wherever God puts us.

Luke's final words capture the spirit of the entire book: *He proclaimed the kingdom of God and taught about the Lord Jesus Christ with all boldness and without hindrance.* The gospel that began in Jerusalem now reached the world's greatest city and kept moving forward. No prison, persecution, or power could stop it. This lesson, along with the book of Acts as a whole, reminds us that the mission continues. God equips each believer to serve faithfully in their own "Rome," wherever that may be. Our task isn't to control the outcome but to stay bold, steady, and surrendered to the Lord who still works "without hindrance."

Memory Verse and Weekly Challenge

He proclaimed the kingdom of God and taught about the Lord Jesus Christ with all boldness and without hindrance.
Acts 28:31 (CSB)

Weekly Challenge: Wherever you are, see it as your mission field. Ask God how you can serve, encourage, or speak for Him today. The gospel advances through daily faith and courage—serve boldly, trusting God to work through you "without hindrance."

For Discussion

1. How did Paul's time on Malta show that God can turn difficulty into opportunity for ministry?

   _____

   _____

   _____

2. What can we learn from Paul's calm faith and servant heart after the shipwreck?

   _____

   _____

   _____

3. Why do you think Paul found such encouragement when he met the believers on the way to Rome?

   _____

   _____

   _____

4. How does Paul's ministry in Rome demonstrate that the gospel cannot be stopped by circumstance?

   _____

   _____

   _____

5. What would it look like for you to serve "with all boldness and without hindrance" in your own daily life?

   _____

   _____

Conclusion

The story of Acts ends, but the mission of Christ continues.

From Jerusalem to Judea, from the stormy seas to the streets of Rome, the book of Acts demonstrates how God's Spirit empowers ordinary people to accomplish extraordinary things. Every chapter shows the same truth: the power of the gospel isn't based on perfect circumstances but on faithful hearts.

Paul's life, especially in these final chapters, exemplifies what it means to live as a servant of Christ. He was misunderstood, opposed, beaten, and imprisoned—yet he was never defeated. He trusted God's promises, served wherever he was placed, and viewed every challenge as an opportunity to glorify Jesus. Whether preaching in a synagogue, defending himself before kings, or encouraging others from a rented house in Rome, Paul lived with one goal: to proclaim the kingdom of God and the name of Christ without fear.

God still works the same way today. The Spirit equips every believer to:

- **Serve faithfully** where they are planted.
- **Endure hardship** with steady trust in God's promises.
- **Shepherd and strengthen others** in faith.
- **Defend the gospel** with humility and courage.
- **Share Christ** with boldness and compassion, "without hindrance."

The mission of Acts has become our mission. The Spirit who empowered the apostles now empowers us. The same grace that sustained Paul sustains every disciple who chooses to live for the kingdom of God.

www.ingramcontent.com/pod-product-compliance
Lightning Source LLC
LaVergne TN
LVHW010320070426
835513LV00025B/2436